D0811294

DOGS

A very peculiar history™

I am I because my little dog
knows me.

Gertrude Stein (1874–1948)

For Jessie

FMacD

Published in Great Britain in MMXIII by
Book House, an imprint of
The Salariya Book Company Ltd
25 Marlborough Place, Brighton BN1 1UB
www.salariya.com
www.book-house.co.uk

HB ISBN-13: 978-1-908973-35-1

1 3 5 7 9 8 6 4 2

A CIP catalogue record for this book is available
from the British Library.

Printed and bound in India.

Printed on paper from sustainable sources.

Visit
www.salariya.com
for our online catalogue and
free interactive web books.

DOGS

A very peculiar history™

Fiona Macdonald

Created and designed by
David Salariya

SALARIYA
BH
BOOK HOUSE

"

What servant loves his master more? What companion more faithful?

Roman natural historian, Lucius Junius Moderatus Columella (AD 4–70)

"

Contents

66

Hounds follow those who
feed them.

Prince Otto von Bismarck (1815–1898)

99

INTRODUCTION

Lions are 'kings of beasts'; horses are swift and strong; cats are aloof and beautiful; apes are intelligent (and our near relatives, also). But the creature closest to most human hearts? Without doubt, the dog!

At first sight, this seems more than a little mysterious. In many languages, 'dog' is a term of great contempt. A grave insult, to a man or woman. Dogs have been called greedy, shameless, lazy, unclean – as in the Biblical condemnation of a persistent sinner or fool: 'like a dog returning to its vomit'. Today, dogs still pollute city streets and carry diseases.

A messy business

In 2005, local government statisticians estimated that dogs deposited 1,000 tonnes of excrement on British streets every day, costing a staggering £22 million pounds every year to clean up.

In July 2012, according to the *News and Star*, a resident of Carlisle, northwest England, was compulsorily escorted out of Carlisle Council Chambers after waving a bag of dog mess at elected members. The protester was complaining about an alleged lack of council street-cleaning services.

Elsewhere, local leaders in New York City decided to use humour as their weapon. They planned a public education programme, urging dog owners to behave responsibly and hygienically. It was launched with the unforgettable slogan: 'There Is No Poop Fairy In East Harlem!'

Hell-hounds

As well as being dirty, in many civilisations, past and present, dogs have been symbols of danger, disorder, death and destruction. Shakespeare's hero, King Henry V, urges his men to 'Cry "Havoc!", and let slip the dogs [the horrors] of war.' We say that a person who has lost all self-respect or self-control has 'gone to the dogs'. And a hopeless case has 'not got a dog's chance'.

For centuries, dogs have been shamefully abused, as a matter of routine. What could be worse than to 'lead a dog's life' or 'die like a dog', cold, starving, alone and scorned, and probably kicked and beaten? A 'dog's dinner' is an awful mess. And 'Black Dog' is a synonym for deepest, direst depression.

Lucky dog!

Yet dogs are also loved – madly, truly, deeply, by millions of adults and children worldwide. (And they are valued, even though that is not exactly the same thing. In 2011, a Chinese industrialist paid $1.5 million for a red Tibetan Mastiff, Hong Dong (Big Splash) – a world record.) Ancient Greek conqueror Alexander the Great (356–323 BC) named a city after his dog Peritas, who died fighting alongside him. Princess Elizabeth, now Queen Elizabeth II, took her favourite Corgi, Susan, on honeymoon with her.

In the USA, hundreds of people every year leave legacies to their dogs – although few go so far as Countess Karlotta Liebenstein, who left over $60 million to her German Shepherd when she died in 1991. The dog's son, or, rather, its trustees, later purchased a luxurious mansion belonging to the singer Madonna. And – although this may just be an urban myth – it is said to be illegal to pull rude faces at a dog in the US state of Oklahoma. In case you hurt its feelings? Newspapers today frequently record examples of owners' extreme devotion to their pet dogs, or feature tug-of-love dog stories, with headlines such as:

Custody battle erupts over Elizabeth Taylor's beloved Maltese terrier.

Daily Mail, 18 April 2012

The hard-rock band Black Sabbath (not renowned for sentimentality) wrote a hit song *Digital Bitch* in praise of a favourite Irish Wolfhound. In 2012, touching photos of a man who carries his elderly, arthritic dog into Lake Superior every night (so that its waters will lull the dog to sleep) appeared on the Internet and quickly went viral. Messages of sympathy and admiration poured in from all round the world, and an anonymous donor offered to pay for specialist treatment to ease the dog's suffering.

In fact, you can pay for all kinds of cosseting for Max and Molly or Jake and Maggie (the most popular dog's names in the USA – they are also, of course, perfectly good names for humans). Dog treats range from yoga and aromatherapy to manicures and massage. You can buy dog playgrounds, dog perfumes and dog clothes for summer with inbuilt cooling pads. In the wintry mountains of Austria, the author once saw a dog dressed in a smart quilted ski-suit. For parties, there are dog-collars decorated with rhinestones or artificial flowers. In Japan, dog owners can display their affluence and taste by shopping at exclusive dog-wear boutiques. One UK dog equipment store named (yes, really) 'Inner Wolf' thoughtfully advertises that dogs are welcome to visit.

In many countries, you can purchase dog life-jackets and boots, dog backpacks, and special dog-containers to fix to the handlebars of your bicycle. Almost every dog garment you can imagine, and more, is available online, ranging from dog tee-shirts and baseball caps to dog sunglasses, dog pyjamas, dog slippers (sold in sets of four!) and dog scarves – bizarrely, made of washable, shaggy false fur. You can even, if you really want, order personalised dog name-tags, plated in 24-carat gold.

You can buy recipe books for dog meals or dog biscuits, send your dog a birthday card, pack it off for a holiday to a fun-filled summer camp and stretch its mind with specially designed dog brain games. You can even have your deceased dog's ashes heat- and pressure-treated to turn them into gemstones. As one fond wearer of sparkling jewellery allegedly explained:

> He was a diamond dog, and now he's a diamond ring…
>
> Quoted in the UK's *Sun* newspaper, 27 April 2012

If canine creatures overburdened with love get depressed or start behaving badly, then there are dog classes or trained animal counsellors to sort out their problems. If a dog gets lonely, in San Diego USA it can watch Dog TV, a cable channel designed to keep dogs 'calm and occupied'. If a beloved dog dies, owners can seek the services of pet-loss therapists.

How many?

• In 2011, there were 78.2 million pet dogs in the USA, plus perhaps half as many abandoned dogs or strays. Around one US household in every three owned a dog. Each dog cost its owner between $600 and $900 in feed and vets' fees.

• In the UK in 2011, there were around 8 million dogs. About one-quarter of all households kept a dog as a pet. Over one-third of pet-owners said that they had replaced a former partner with a dog, cat, bird, fish or small furry mammal.

• In Europe in 2011, there were over 73 million dogs. This included 12.5 million in Russia. Dogs were one-quarter of the European pet population.

• European sales of pet food in 2011 totalled 8 million tonnes, and generated a turnover for petfood manufacturers of around €24 million.

• Pet-based industries (including veterinary care) in Europe employed around 550,000 people in 2011.

• In 2011, veterinary scientists estimated that there were around 525 million dogs in the world. Economists say that their number is rising fast, as developing countries – China, India, Brazil, Russia – and also Japan, begin to follow a more affluent lifestyle.

Dogs – presented as they are, or sentimentally loaded with human virtues and qualities – have featured in countless myths, legends, narratives, fictions, jokes, films, games and sayings. Yet the history of their relationship with our own species has not always been happy. Read on, and find out more.

66

Listen to them – the
children of the night. What
music they make!

Bram Stoker, *Dracula*, 1897

99

CHAPTER ONE

ONCE A WOLF...

Few people who have read Bram Stoker's classic vampire novel *Dracula* – or seen the films inspired by it – will forget the nightmare journey made by the story's innocent young hero towards Dracula's castle. He travels in darkness, through wild, mountainous countryside. A full moon sails across scudding black clouds, ghostly flames flicker and die, and the traveller's coach, complete with demonic driver, is surrounded by 'a ring of wolves, with white teeth and lolling red tongues, with long, sinewy limbs and shaggy hair'. The young hero experiences 'a sort of paralysis of fear. It is only when a man feels himself face to face with such horrors that he can understand their true import [= significance].'

Bram Stoker does not tell his readers what the 'true import' of the wolf-pack was. He did not need to. In the nineteenth century, and for hundreds of years before, wolves were indeed the 'children of the night', the man-eating animal embodiment of evil.

Hated and feared

Wild wolves had been hated and feared ever since humans first kept tasty sheep, goats and cattle conveniently gathered together in fields or pens near their villages, ready for predators, such as wolves, to attack. Settled farming developed at different times and in different places, but the earliest known evidence of villages with domesticated livestock dates from around 11,000 years ago, and comes from the Middle East.

Thousands of years later, ancient Greeks and Romans told thrilling stories about wolf-men monsters, and created myths with moral messages that featured 'savage' wolves. In Viking and Saxon northern Europe, warriors dressed in wolf-skins to frighten their enemies and fight more ferociously. The medieval Christian Church taught that excommunicated men and women (people banned from the Church's holy rituals, and thereby damned to eternal punishment in Hell) might turn into werewolves. The folktale of *Red Riding Hood* identified wolves with wild and fatal sexuality. Bram Stoker's *Dracula* borrowed from European folklore that linked wolves and vampires; across the Atlantic, settlers and ranchers in the new USA declared war on the wolves that killed their cattle. By the mid-20th century, wolves were almost extinct in many parts of the world.

But times change. Almost as soon as we realised that wolves might not be with us for much longer, we came to value the same wildness in them that had horrified earlier generations. Today wolves have become romantic, even glamorous. They are symbols of the glorious untamed freedom of the natural world, and/or tragic victims of thoughtless humanity that is trashing the planet. We can see wolves portrayed positively in films, most famously, perhaps, in Kevin Costner's *Dances with Wolves* (1990); we can visit wolf sanctuaries, go on wolf safaris, adopt a wolf, keep one as a (dangerous) pet, play computer games featuring menacing wolf monsters, download wolf-howl ringtones, and even take part in wolf-howling competitions.

Just the one

Why all this information about wolves? Because, not long after wolves had been rehabilitated as noble, rather than vicious, savages, scientists discovered that all the dogs in the world today were descended from just one wild species: *Canis lupus* (grey or gray wolf). Of course, people had suspected for centuries that dogs and wolves were closely linked. But dogs came in so many different shapes and sizes (see page 52) that it seemed impossible to believe that they all shared exactly the same forefathers and mothers – although the most perceptive observers of the animal kingdom thought that this must be so:

if...it could be shown that the greyhound, bloodhound, terrier, spaniel and bull-dog, which we all know propagate their kind truly, were the offspring of any single species, then such facts would have great weight in making us doubt about the immutability of the many closely allied natural species...

Charles Darwin, *On The Origin Of Species*, 1859

propagate their kind truly: produce pups that are exactly like their parents
immutability: unchangeability.

Darwin was hoping that dogs all shared the same ancestor because it would prove his theory of natural selection – that living things could change and develop over time, to fit themselves to their changing environments. He would doubtless have been delighted when, in 1997, experts in genetics, studying mitochondrial DNA (genetic material passed from mothers to their offspring), showed that theory was correct. Dogs big and small, smooth and hairy, fast or slow, were ALL descended from grey wolves (*Canis lupus*), and no other species.

So! The wolf's ancestry is the ancestry of the domestic dog, as well. It's a long story...

How scientists classify dogs

Kingdom: Animalia
Phylum: Chordata
Class: Mammalia
Order: Carnivora
Suborder: Caniformia
Family: Canidae
Subfamily: Caninae
Genus: Canis
Species: *Canis lupus*
Subspecies: *Canis lupus familiaris*

As a simple reference, a kingdom is the largest and oldest main group; a subspecies is the smallest and newest.

Meat-eaters

Dogs, wolves and over 30 other species living in the world today belong to the biological family Canidae. Like all other members of the order Carnivora (meat-eaters), they have pairs of curved carnassial (shear-like) teeth. All Carnivora are descended from small, furry, weasel-like, tree-climbing mammals called Miacids, who evolved 50 to 60 million years ago. Ideas about dog evolution are changing all the time, as new fossils are discovered or old ones re-examined. But you can see one possible family tree for wolves and dogs on page 24.

Cats and dogs

By around 42 million years ago, the Miacids had evolved into two very different kinds of creatures: the suborder Feliformia (or Feloidea), who were the ancestors of all cats, and the suborder Caniformia (or Canoidea), who were the ancestors of wolves, bears, seals, sea lions, walruses, racoons, weasels – and dogs. All Caniformia have long muzzles; most have claws that cannot be retracted (pulled back into their paws).

Genetic ancestry of today's dogs

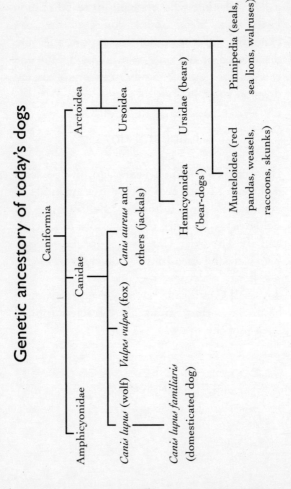

Teeth and claws

In North America, between 42 and 32 million years ago, some members of the Canifornia suborder developed into a new family, the Canidae. Scientists divide the Canidae into three branches, called subfamilies:

• **Hesperocyoninae** ('Western Dogs', because one of the best fossil examples was found in Texas, USA). They mostly lived in the grasslands in North America.

• **Borophaginae** ('Bone-Crushers'). This numbered an astonishing 66 different species, from small tree-climbers to huge meat-eaters the size of bears. With powerful teeth and jaws, borophaginae were often the top predators within their local ecosystems.

• **Caninae** ('Dogs') This subfamily did not evolve until around 34–32 million years ago, but it is still going strong. It's the only branch of the Canidae still surviving today, and includes wolves, foxes, coyotes, jackals and domestic dogs.

Towards a dog

The earliest Western Dog yet discovered, **Protohesperocyon**, lived around 42 million years ago. It was about the size of a pine marten, with a fairly short muzzle, flexible tail and strong body. It could still climb trees, and mostly survived by eating birds, eggs, insects, fruits and seeds. But it had evolved longer legs than its Miacid ancestors, and these made it better suited to running and chasing prey on the ground. It also had pads on its paws to protect its feet while running. Although Protohesperocyon was not a direct ancestor of modern dogs, it shows us the way in which early Canidae were evolving to become more doglike.

A blind alley?

By around 33 million years ago, the first creature that we might recognise as a dog evolved: **Archaeocyon** ('Beginning Dog'). It belonged to the **Borophaginae** (Bone-Crusher) subfamily. 'Beginning Dog' was small, typically weighing only 1.4 kg.

However, it looked rather doglike, and its teeth show that it consumed not only meat but a wide range of plant and animal foods, as modern dogs do today.

However, many other Bone-Crusher species were not so well adapted for survival in a diverse range of habitats. Over the years, they grew larger, stronger, longer-legged and very good at chasing other animals – typically, primitive antelope, horses and camels. They used their sharp carnassial teeth to tear flesh (and swallow chunks whole), and ate very little else. However, when the world's climate changed and their large, meaty prey species dwindled, the big Bone-Crushers went hungry, and died out.

Side by side

In the past, scientists used to think that modern wolves and dogs were descended from the Bone-Crushers, especially (as its name suggests) from Archaeocyon (Beginning Dog). But recent re-examination of fossil skull-bones has led experts to discount this theory. They think, instead, that wolves and dogs share a common ancestor (Caniformia) with Bone-Crushers and Western Dogs, but are not descended from them. They belong to a separate but closely related subfamily that evolved alongside: the **Caninae**.

The most likely ancestor of wolves and dogs appeared on earth while the Bone-Crushers were still growing bigger and more specialised (about 32 million years ago). But it turned out to be a much, much better survivor.

Just what was this cleverly adapted creature? Named **Leptocyon** (small, thin dog), it was smaller and more agile and graceful than the big, brute Bone-Crushers. It weighed around 4 kg; the size of a very large cat. It had longish legs, a long tail, and a long muzzle. *Leptocyon* survived for over 20 million years (from around 32 to 11 million years ago), making it one of the most enduring creatures ever to have lived on this planet. Unlike the Bone-Crushers, it was not a specialised top predator, relying for food on a narrow range of prey that lived in one particular environment. Instead, it was able to make the best of all possible chances of survival. *Leptocyon* proved that it could thrive while the bigger, stronger Bone-Crushers became extinct. Why? Mostly because (like modern dogs) it was prepared to vary its diet and eat almost anything: birds, lizards, rabbits, insects, berries and leaves, shoots and roots of all kinds.

Foxes, jackals, coyotes, wolves...

Leptocyon finally became extinct around 11 million years ago, not long after some of its relatives had evolved into a whole new branch of the Caninae subfamily: the tribe (sub-subfamily) *Vulpini*. These were the ancestors of modern foxes; from around 12 million years ago, foxes evolved quite separately from wolves and dogs.

At around the same time, direct descendants of *Leptocyon* had themselves evolved again, into the genus **Eucyon** (Original Dog), a medium-size (9 kg) running, hunting, creature that ate a wide variety of foods. Rather confusingly, to modern eyes, *Eucyon* still looked like a fox, but its legs were extremely long, and its skull was clearly different from all the true foxes. The bones of its nose suggest that it had a much keener sense of smell than its ancestors; this helped it hunt in packs with others of its kind, like modern wolves. Its teeth had evolved as well, to become similar to those of modern dogs.

Around 6 million years ago, *Eucyon*'s descendants evolved into another new genus. This was ***Canis*** – the ancestors of wolves, coyotes, jackals, and dogs. It had all *Eucyon*'s evolutionary advantages, and more.

Round the world

Until around 9 million years ago, all members of the Caninae subfamily lived only in North America. But during repeated Ice Ages, the world's seas became frozen ice sheets, leaving large areas of the sea-bed uncovered to act as land bridges. Two of the most important linked Alaska and Siberia (across the Bering Strait, at various times between 55 million and around 12,000 years ago) and North and

South America (at Panama, around 3 million years ago). *Eucyon* travelled from America to Asia around 9 million years ago, across these land bridges. Then, between 6 and 3.5 million years ago, it was followed by several different members of the new *Canis* genus.

This migration by *Eucyon* and then *Canis* coincided with climate and environmental change (the forests of North America became drier grasslands) and with the evolution of large herds of hoofed animals that fed on grass. As these creatures travelled in search of food, *Eucyon* and *Canis* followed them. By now, *Canis* was larger and stronger. It had the stamina to chase herd animals, catch them, drag them down and devour them.

Fossil remains of *Canis* have been found in Asia, Europe and Africa dating from around 6 million to 3.5 million years ago. A large – and bewildering – variety of *Canis* subspecies developed in all three continents, each adapted to local food supplies and the local environment.

Going back home

By around 1.8 million years ago, *Canis* were becoming increasingly like modern wolves. Still following herds, it began to spread back across the Bering Strait land bridge, finally spreading right though North America around 150,000–100,000 years ago.

The latest models

After 60 million years of growth, change and adaptation, the first species of modern wolves evolved in Europe about one million years ago, from *Canis* ancestors. Named *Canis etruscus*, it was soon followed by *C. mosbachensis*. By around 300,000 years ago, *C. mosbachensis* had developed into the species *C. lupus*, the fierce grey wolf known to modern humans and portrayed in countless stories and superstitions. For a long time, from around 11,000 BC to AD 1500, the grey wolf became the most widespread predator on the planet. Now, although persecuted in some countries, it still survives.

Here they are!

And what of dogs? No-one is one-hundred-percent certain. But recent theories, based on genetics, claim that they developed as a subspecies of the grey wolf around 130,000–140,000 years ago. Over the centuries, many different subspecies of *C. lupus* interbred (there are many other subspecies of grey wolves still alive, in every continent except Antarctica), creating a rich genetic mixture. Scientists have identified four separate ancient clades (genetic groups) among grey wolves, from the Middle East, the Himalaya region, India and the Arctic. They cannot agree as to which was the most likely ancestor of modern dogs – but, whichever it was, its descendants have proved highly successful. Today known as *Canis lupus familiaris*, the dog is here to stay!

66

…at the present day there
is hardly a tribe so
barbarous, as not to have
domesticated at least
the dog…

Charles Darwin, *On the Origin of Species*, 1859

99

CHAPTER TWO

YOU CAN'T TEACH AN OLD DOG NEW TRICKS

I f you were a Stone-Age mother with a young baby, living at any time between around 135,000 BC and 60,000 BC, how would you keep your child clean, dry and comfortable? You might use moss as a nappy, perhaps, but what if there was none to be found near your camp? You might possibly dunk your infant in a fast-flowing stream – quite pleasant in summer, but a chiller-killer in wintertime. You don't have cloth – it hasn't been invented yet – and neither animal hides nor dried leaves seem to fit the bill. What you need (and I apologise to readers with delicate stomachs), yes, what you need is a dog.

A hungry, greedy, biddable, licking dog. A dog with a gentle nature and a long, damp tongue. And, quite possibly, you have one – or more.

How did this happen? As watchful, presumably loving, parents, prehistoric people were not going to risk their babies' lives by letting big fierce wolves anywhere near them. So the animal they entrusted with their babies' intimate hygiene must either have been very friendly and docile, or else reliably obedient – or both. In other words, it must have been tamed and domesticated; used not only to living alongside humans but also to co-operating with them.

I may be tame but I'm not domestic!

If they could talk, that's what several members of wild species might say. Today, as in the past, individual animals and birds that would normally live a wild, free lifestyle occasionally allow themselves to be befriended by a patient and sympathetic human. Famous examples include the otters that lived with Scottish author Gavin Maxwell (*Ring of Bright Water*) or Elsa the lioness, who formed a close relationship with Joy Adamson, author of *Born Free*.

A tamed animal might easily 'go back to the wild' if its special human contact disappears. But a domesticated animal is something very different. It is a species or subspecies that has developed genetically, through natural selection or artificial breeding, to lead a lifestyle that is closely interrelated with humans and may even depend on them. Natural selection produces animals that are tolerant of human company. Breeding produces animals with characteristics that humans like, need or admire.

Today, we also have 'feral' animals: creatures that are genetically domestic but which have moved away from a lifestyle involving humans. In many parts of the world, there are large and sometimes dangerous packs of feral dogs.

Transformation

Dogs were the very first animals to be domesticated by humans. We know (see page 20) that dogs are genetically very close to grey wolves. But how did this happen? And when?

Alas, dear readers, nobody knows with absolute certainty. In the same way, no-one knows whether wolf domestication occurred just once or multiple times across the Northern Hemisphere. But most experts think that the wolf was transformed into a domestic dog several times and at several different places, including China, Europe and the Middle East.

Adopt-a-puppy

One of the oldest ideas about wolf domestication is also the most charming. It supposes that early hunter-gatherer humans came across some cuddly, fluffy wolf-cubs, took them home, fed them, kept them warm, petted them, and gave them to the children to play with. In time, more cubs were born and grew up to become part of the human family. They helped with tracking and hunting. They guarded the camp. They became dogs.

It's a nice picture. But scientists who study modern wolves say that it simply could not have happened. Where would early hunter-gatherers find milk to feed the wolf puppies? (Sheep, cows, goats and all other farm animals were domesticated after dogs, not before them.) No modern trainer has been able to tame a wolf that was parted from its mother at more than 21 days old, and puppies younger than that are physically very fragile. After 21 days, wolf pups begin to learn defensive behaviours from their parents, and genes that affect their character (especially for fierceness) begin to mould their brains. By nature, wild wolves are shy and wary; they do not willingly interact with humans.

Even if wolf pups could be easily tamed, where would busy hunter-gatherers find the time to care for wolf puppies? As anyone who has watched a bitch rear a litter will know, dog motherhood is a round-the-clock, full-time occupation.

The silver fox experiment

In 1959, no-one had yet proved that dogs were descended from wolves. But top Russian geneticist Dmitry K. Belyaev planned an experiment to discover whether close relatives of wolves – silver foxes – could be not just tamed but fully domesticated by careful selective breeding.

Yes, they could! After 40 years, some of Belyaev's foxes had become so well adapted to human company that they cuddled up to their carers and licked their faces, just like dogs. At the same time, they showed physical changes found in modern dogs and other domesticated creatures. These included smaller size than their wild relatives, longer childhoods, white 'stars' in their fur, long shaggy coats, and curly tails. If this could happen to foxes, had it happened to wolves, also?

Getting closer...

The oldest archaeological evidence of dog domestication comes from around 33,000 years ago. And it shows quite clearly that dog-like creatures and early humans were living close together. In 2010, the fossil jaw bones and skull of an 'almost' dog (nicknamed 'Razbo') were excavated in southern Siberia. It had lived close to camps of hunter-gatherer people, but perhaps became extinct during the Last Glacial Maximum (extreme cold period) around 26,500–19,000 years ago. The excavators who found it suggest that similar dogs were also evolving elsewhere, and that some of them had survived to become the ancestors of all our dogs today.

Hug-a-puppy?

In Europe, doglike fossils have been found in caves where there are clear traces of human activity, for example at Goyet Cave in Belgium, dating from around 31,700 years ago, and at Chauvet Cave in France, where footprints of a boy and a dog who lived about

26,000 years ago have been preserved not far from one another.

In 2011, the skeleton of a 26,000- to 27,000-year-old 'almost' dog was found in the Czech Republic. It had been buried with a hole drilled in its skull; among early peoples, this was often done to let the spirits of the dead escape. Early humans had also placed a mammoth bone in its mouth, perhaps to sustain it as it travelled through the afterlife. Examples of jewellery made of dog-teeth were found nearby. This creature clearly had some kind of relationship with – or maybe even magic status among – the people who handled its body after death. Presumably, while it was alive, they had loved or respected it. But we don't know for sure whether it was domesticated, or simply tamed.

Archaeologists have found the remains of dogs and humans deliberately buried together about 14,000 years ago in Germany, at Bonn-Oberkassel. In Palestine, around 12,000 years ago, an elderly woman was buried holding a puppy in her arms.

Survival of the friendliest

The excavators of 'Razbo' suggest that dog domestication first took place when environmental conditions were favourable (temperate climate, grazing land, animals to prey on) and when wolves who wanted to be friendly with humans found humans who were willing to befriend them. Very probably, this happened slowly, step by step:

• Some time after around 6 million years ago, wolves group themselves together in packs to hunt. It takes a long, long time, but they evolve social skills: observing fellow pack members, communicating, interacting and co-operating with them.

• Some time between 150,000 and 100,000 years ago, a few wolves get used to early human hunters. They no longer run or hide when they see people, and begin to hang around human camps, maybe eating refuse or human waste, or catching wounded animals escaping from human hunters. Evolution favours the friendliest: the wolves who spend longest close to humans get most food.

• At the same time, wolves begin to observe humans, and look for signals from them. In an experiment in 2002, scientists showed that wolf puppies were better than chimpanzees at noticing and interpreting human behaviour. Wolves and people are also two of the few species to communicate using eye signals.

• Early people find that wolves can be useful. By eating refuse, wolves keep camp sites cleaner. Wolf barks warn of approaching danger. Most humans leave the scavenging wolves to live as they choose, but perhaps some humans begin to feed them. Perhaps this is when the first wild wolves become tamed by humans.

• Wolves and people develop and change together. Humans learn from wolves to hunt in large groups, and chase big wild creatures such as mammoths. As they hunt, humans develop the communication skills needed to work with each other – and with wolves and dogs. Human and wolf social systems now have several similar features.

• If these 'adapted' wolves have puppies, they will grow up surrounded by humans. They will be less fearful of human contact. They may even learn to join in human hunting expeditions. Their development from puppies to adults will be delayed (like the Russian silver foxes, page 40), giving them more time to observe humans, grow more friendly and less fearful, and learn to interact with them.

• Wolves are not yet domesticated, but they are getting close to it. It's only when early humans begin to select wolves and pups with 'desirable' characteristics (less aggressive, more co-operative) and encourage them to breed, that the first domesticated wolves appear.

• Between 40,000 and 15,000 years ago, the first domesticated dogs and 'almost' dogs are living with humans. We can see the fossil evidence.

• Between 14,000 and 10,000 years ago, humans start to live as farmers. At the same time, dogs slowly became smaller, with a smaller brain than wild wolves. They develop a 'stop' in the bone-structure between their eyes and their nose – perhaps the beginning of short-muzzled dogs. Unlike wolf-mothers, female dogs do not regurgitate their food to feed their puppies. This suggests that dogs have found a regular food supply, and rely on humans to provide it.

Prehistoric new technology – the dog!

It's not a machine – it's a living and breathing dog. However, so some experts say, it has made just as great an impact on human life as the wheel or the computer.

• Groups of early humans living with early dogs had big advantages over rival human communities. The 'dog people' got more food, because dogs helped with hunting. Their camps (and babies) were cleaner, healthier and better guarded. Humans may also have trained dogs to carry heavy loads, sparing themselves effort and leaving their own hands free for other tasks.

• Wolves were domesticated at around the same time as modern humans (*Homo sapiens sapiens*) were replacing a rival human subspecies, the Neanderthals *(H. neanderthalensis)*. Perhaps the hunting, cleaning guarding, carrying dog was *H. sapiens*'s 'secret weapon', helping them, not the Neanderthals, to survive and take over the planet.

• It has even been argued that the presence of dogs helped humans invent a new weapon: bow and arrows. An arrow can fly much further than a spear hurled by a human. But if the human cannot find the prey his arrow has killed, it is no use to him. However, a dog can run fast to follow wounded prey, or use its keen sense of smell and tracking instinct to find it.

"

Bulldogs are adorable, with faces like toads that have been sat on.

French novelist Sidonie-Gabrielle Colette (1873–1954)

The hair of the dog [that bit you].

Popular name for a hangover cure, and before that, a famous – but useless – remedy for rabies.

"

CHAPTER THREE

DOGSBODY

Nickname for a dutiful, hard-working person,
obeying orders from a superior

P eople in the past had some very, very
strange ideas about dogs' bodies. According to
Greek physician Hippocrates (lived around
400 BC, and still famous as 'the Father
of Medicine'), 'the flesh of dogs is of
a heating, drying, and corroborating
(reinforcing) nature'. For thousands of years,
dogs' hair, dogs' teeth, dogs' blood and
even dogs' excrement were all used in cures.
Eating dogs' flesh formed part of black magic
rituals that aimed to bring the dead back to
life. In ancient Egypt, male dogs' genitals were
reputed to stop dark hair going grey.

In the European Middle Ages, churchman and scholar Gerald of Wales wrote that the tongue of the dog possessed healing qualities. Christian preachers in Italy told how St Roch, suffering from plague, was cured when a dog licked his sores. Medieval bestiaries (books about real or fabulous animals, with a strongly moral message) claimed that the body of a young dog, tied to a sick person, could absorb the 'poison' that was causing their disease.

Turning to dogs themselves, the ancient Romans believed that rabies (a deadly disease) could be prevented by cutting off dogs' tails, or cured by removing a (non-existent) 'worm' from underneath their tongues. Given that rabies was passed to humans by dog-bites, and was always fatal, this cure sounds quite frighteningly dangerous for the person wielding the knife.

Nearer to our own times, English women in the seventeenth century wishing for beautiful complexions used 'puppy water', distilled from the bodies of newborn baby dogs. Why such heartless murder? Following Hippocrates, would-be beauties thought that puppy-fat had a particular power to calm and soften skin. They also favoured gloves made of dog-hide; it was supposed to be smoothing, and a reliable barrier to sunlight. Soft, white hands were a sign of nobility, and much admired.

In the late 18th century, French Emperor Napoleon cut both ears off his dog Sambo, simply for the sake of fashion. By the time that celebrated French author Colette was writing about bulldogs, soon after 1900, breeders were creating designer dogs with (perhaps) 'adorable' but definitely unhealthily exaggerated features.

Today, we have mercifully stopped using puppy-water, although dog flesh is still eaten in some countries (see reference to Bok-Nal on page 189) as food, rather than for magic purposes, and several wild *Canis* species and subspecies are still hunted to use in traditional medicine or for other superstitious reasons. (In Bolivia, for example, sitting on the pelt of a wild wolf is said to bring cowboys good luck.) Irresponsible breeders, and the owners who buy their output, continue to be the cause of suffering among dogs. Thanks to modern science, however, we do now know much more than past peoples about dogs' bodies and how they work.

From nose to tail

For a single subspecies, *Canis lupus familiaris* (dog) displays an extraordinary range of shapes and sizes. No other mammal shows greater diversity. However, from the tallest Wolfhounds and Great Danes or the most massive St Bernards (which can weigh 115 kg) to the tiniest Chihuahuas (weighing 1 kg – that's over one hundred times lighter), all dogs share the same basic anatomy. A small book like this can't hope to be comprehensive, but let's take a quick tour of man's best friend to see some highlights of the canine body.

From the cradle to the grave

In the wild, wolves breed only once a year. But domestic dogs are capable of mating in winter and summer. A typical canine pregnancy lasts for 63 days. Litter size depends on weight and height. The smaller the dog, the smaller the number of puppies. Taking all the breeds together, a litter of around 7 puppies is the average.

All puppies are born blind and deaf. They use their sense of smell to locate their mother and feed. Dog's milk is very rich and tastes sweet. Its concentrated nourishment helps puppies grow fast, but most adult dogs lose the ability to digest milk – drinking it can make them ill.

The kindness of strangers

In a tragic story that might perhaps give affluent dog-owners pause for thought, a UK newspaper reported in July 2012 that a starving boy from eastern India had been seen drinking milk from a friendly feral dog.

Chotu said: 'Our family is very poor, sometimes I get hungry.'

The Sun, July 2012

Puppy love

Puppies' eyes (always blue) open after around 12 days. At around the same time, their ears – which are flat to the side of their heads at first – begin to grow large and floppy or stand up in 'pricked' position, depending on the breed. The channel leading from the outer ear to the eardrum also begins to open, and, for the first time, puppies can hear.

Puppies' milk teeth begin to break through their gums at 4 weeks after birth. By the time they are 6 weeks old, they can eat solid food. Many breeders let pups move to a new home at 10–12 weeks (and many mother dogs are relieved to see them go). However, unlike wolves, young dogs are able to transfer their puppy affections to new humans until they are 4 months old or more. By that time their eyes will usually have turned brown, the normal adult colour. At 4 months, puppies begin to grow adult teeth, and lose their baby ones.

The age at which dogs become fully grown varies from around 9–12 months for toy dogs to 18 months for larger ones. The average dog's lifespan is around 13 years, if they are lucky. But larger dogs often have shorter lives, and smaller dogs can live for much longer. Growing quickly puts stress on a large dog's bones and muscles. So do years of moving a big, heavy body around. Scientists also suggest that, in order to grow so big so quickly, large dogs are genetically programmed with 'speeded up' development. Genes for extra-fast growth also make it likely that a big dog will develop diseases of old age while still quite young.

It is often said that we can calculate how old a dog would be in human years by multiplying its age by 7. This is not strictly true. Not only do big dogs age faster than small ones, but all dogs develop at a different rate from humans. In particular, they mature much more quickly. For example, a one-year old dog from a small to medium breed is at about the same stage in its life-cycle as a teenage human.

Top dogs

• The tallest dog alive today is a Great Dane, Giant George, from the USA. It measures 1.9 metres (44 in.) at the shoulders.

• The longest dog on record is Farrell, an Irish Wolfhound, also from the USA. In 2010, it measured an amazing 2.37 metres (93 in.) from the tip of its nose to the end of its tail.

• The smallest known living dog also comes from the US. A Chihuahua named Booboo, it is just 10.16 cm (4 in.) tall.

• We have to look to the UK to find the dog with the loudest bark. It's Daz, a German Shepherd from Essex, who recorded 108 decibels in 2009. That's not too far from the sound level that causes permanent ear damage in humans (120 db).

• Also from the UK, a mastiff bitch called Tia holds the record for the largest number of puppies in one litter. In 2004, she gave birth to 24 – and 20 survived.

• Chaser, a collie from the USA, is maybe the world's most intelligent dog, or perhaps the best-educated. In 2011, it was said to have a vocabulary of 1,022 words.

• The oldest known dog was Bluey, an Australian Cattle Dog. He passed away in 1939, at the grand old age of 29.

Snorting with pleasure

Dogs sneeze, like humans – they also get hay fever and other allergies – but the loud snorting sound that they often make when pleased, excited or pulling on their leads is something different. Snorting dogs are trying to force air into, not out, of their noses. But the soft palate at the back of their mouth sometimes goes into spasm, making it difficult for the dog to inhale. To compensate, the dog stands still and stretches its head forward as far as it can, panting and snorting.

Extrasensory!

Cold and wet or warm and dry, a dog's nose is one of its most important organs. (It's also unique: for dogs, a noseprint is as individual as a human fingerprint.) The section of a dog's brain that processes smells is 40 times larger than the equivalent area in humans. A dog's nose and nasal passages are lined with a wrinkled, folded lining, about the size of a pocket handkerchief, which contains around 220 million scent receptors.

The dog's whiskers?

Dog muzzles can be long or short, broad or thin, but they all have whiskers sprouting beside the upper lip, on the chin, and above the eyes. Even puppies have them. Whiskers are twice as thick as ordinary hairs, with roots set three times deeper. Compared with cats' magnificent moustaches, dogs' whiskers may look insignificant, but they are just as sensitive to touch as (for example) human fingertips. Dogs use their whiskers to detect small movements of air. This helps them to navigate, even in low light conditions. Whiskers also serve as a warning system: touching the whiskers above the eyes will cause a dog to blink to protect the delicate eyeball from harm. As extra protection, dogs have a third eyelid that slides horizontally across. We rarely see it, unless the dog is asleep or ill. And the average dog sleeps around 12 hours a day, sometimes more!

Giving them the eye

Shepherds, farmers and owners of herding dogs will all recognise that particular moment when the dog senses a group of the animals it has evolved – or been bred – to organise. It will lower its head, flatten its body, point its nose towards the sheep, goats or cattle in question, and glare, glare, glare.

Dogs' eyes have evolved to look forwards, like other predator species. In small, short-muzzled breeds, such as Pekingese, the eyeball is pushed far forward. In larger breeds, with long muzzles, the eyes appear to be sunk more deeply into the dog's skull. But wherever they are placed, dogs' eyes enable them to focus on prey in three dimensions and across a wide angle of view: around 240 degrees. This helps them track and follow prey on the run. It also makes it hard to creep up on dogs from behind without being seen!

Unlike humans, dogs cannot see bright colours or distinguish between red and green; they mostly see in various shades of purple, blue and grey. However, compared with humans, dogs can see much better in dim light. Like cats, they have a reflective screen, the *tapetum lucidum*, behind the retina (layer of light-sensitive cells at the back of the eye). This screen reflects all available light back to the retina – and shines with a ghostly glow when your pet is out of doors late at night.

Shapes and faces

In 2010, Italian scientists asked their research helpers – all dog-owners – to walk to and fro wearing big paper bags over their heads. Why? This was part of an experiment designed to explore how closely dogs related to their owners. In particular, the scientists aimed to discover whether dogs could actually recognise their owners' faces. Readers, be reassured. Dogs definitely do know who loves and feeds them. The researchers found that, when owners' faces were covered with the paper bags, dogs were much, much less likely to respond to them.

Hear, hear

In the wild, wolves and dogs rely on close communication with other members of their pack to survive. Dogs can hear a wider range of sounds than humans, from a low, buzzing 16 hz frequency to supersonic 45 khz. They can also hear noises that are quieter than the human ear can detect, and sounds from four times further away. To achieve this long-distance listening, dogs can move each ear separately (using 18 separate muscles!) to catch faint noises and get a 'fix' on their place of origin.

My, what big teeth you've got...

Yes, just like their ancestors, dogs have fangs. Long, strong, pointed teeth to bite their prey – and hold on. But because dogs are descended from creatures that ate a wide range of foods, they also have teeth that have evolved to crush and grind bones and plant materials. Modern adult dogs have 42 teeth, 20 on the top jaw and 22 on the bottom:

- **12 incisors** = the little teeth right at the front of the mouth, used for gripping and ripping.
- **4 canines** = fangs, used to bite and tear.
- **16 premolars** or **carnassials**, used to cut and crunch, like shears.
- **10 molars,** at the back of the mouth, used to crush and grind.

Wolfing it down

Most dogs have very healthy appetites – obesity is a growing canine problem, as well as a human one. In 2011, an American animal welfare organisation estimated that maybe half of all pet dogs were overweight.

Compared with humans, dogs have very few taste buds: around 1,700, clustered around the tip of the tongue. Dogs can sense the four basic tastes: sweet, sour, salt and bitter. But perhaps it is fear of famine that drives so many to eat as much as they can. Dogs use their tongue to drink, curving the tip into a spoon shape to lift water into their mouths.

Dogs' dinner bell

In a world-famous experiment, in 1901, Russian psychologist Ivan Pavlov (1849–1936) showed how dogs could be conditioned (trained) to salivate, as a reflex (unconscious) action. Every time Pavlov fed his dogs, a bell rang loudly.

At first, the dogs produced saliva at the sight of their food, as part of the normal process of digestion. But Pavlov found that, after a while, they would also salivate just at the sound of the bell, even though no food was being offered to them.

In hot pants ...

A dog is covered in layers of hair, which have evolved to insulate the dog's body from heat and from cold. This means that dogs cannot control their body temperature – on average, 100.5°F to 102.5°F (38°C to 39.2°C) – by evaporating moisture through the skin. Dogs have sweat glands only on their nose and paws.

Instead, dogs keep cool by panting: they open their mouths wide and breathe more heavily and much faster than usual. (At rest, a dog normally breathes between 10 and 32 times per minute.) Panting exchanges hot air from inside a dog's body with cooler air from outside, and pushes warm moisture out from the lungs. This evaporates as it flows out of the dog, and provides extra cooling.

The acid test

Once a dog has swallowed food or drink, this passes into its stomach, washed down by saliva. Like humans', dogs' stomachs contain a strong acid plus digestive enzymes. Together, they break down food so the nutrients it contains can be absorbed into the body. Dogs' food can be raw, tough, fibrous or fatty, and may stay in the stomach for up to 10 or 12 hours.

Give the dog a bone?

In 2012, scientists suggested that dogs' habit of chewing bones evolved between eight and ten million years ago, when their ancestors first started to hunt large animals. To make use of all possible nourishment in massive prey, dog ancestors learned to gnaw all the bits of food that they could not rip or tear or swallow. The canine habit of burying bones was another survival strategy. After a big kill, it was a way of hiding food from rival predator species and storing any surplus for future consumption.

Off the menu

For animals that are classed as 'omnivores' – carnivores that eat everything – a surprising number of foods are very bad for dogs, and some are dangerously toxic. Dog poisons include:

Raisins
Grapes
Avocados
Coffee
Chocolate
Milk
Mushrooms
Onions
Garlic
Apple and pear pips

Sugar, raw meat, eggs or fish, and mouldy or rotten food are also not advisable. Sugar causes overweight and diabetes; raw and rotting foods can harbour dangerous bacteria. Fruit with large stones, such as peaches or cherries, can cause intestinal blockage.

Designed to run

An average dog has a skeleton with 319 bones and over 500 muscles. The most important muscle is the heart, which pumps oxygen-rich blood around the body. Large dogs' hearts beat 60–100 times per minute: small dogs' heart rate is faster, at around 100–140 beats. The skeleton protects a dog's vital organs (brain, heart, digestive system) and supports the dog's skin and muscles. Around 75% of a dog's weight is carried at the front of its body, on its shoulder joints. Unlike humans, dogs do not have collarbones; their front legs are attached to shoulderblades, which are held in place by ligaments, muscles and tendons that link them to the backbone. These 'free' forelegs give a dog great flexibility, and allow a long stride when leaping or running. The huge muscles in a dog's back legs provide the power to push it forward.

Most dogs have stamina, rather than speed: a wolf can run all day, but at only around 5 miles per hour. Dogs bred to run fast, such as greyhounds, have unusually light bone structure, huge hearts, and a higher percentage of 'fast-twitch' muscles (used for acceleration) than other dogs. Greyhounds also have a 'double-suspension gait'. At full speed, their legs are fully stretched – forwards and backwards at the same time. On the next stride, the legs fold over each other, so the back paws are in front of the forepaws.

Normal dogs move in a bewildering number of ways, depending on the size and shape of the dog's body, the length of its legs, and the speed at which it is travelling. However, all dogs run, walk, bound and leap on the tips of their toes. A dog has five toes on each front foot, including a dew-claw, which is positioned and sometimes used rather like a human thumb. Most dogs have four claws on each back foot; a few breeds have back dew-claws, as well. Claws and rough footpads (the thickest skin on a dog's body) provide grip on rough or muddy surfaces; the pads act as cushioned shock-absorbers. A small carpal pad, higher up the dog's leg, helps the dog stay stable when it is on a slope, or sliding. Dogs' feet have a thick covering of hair, and a special circulation of blood that stops flesh and skin freezing at temperatures down to –35°C.

Right at the end of our anatomical tour, the tail is one of the dog's most remarkable features. It can be straight or curled, short or long, with between 6 and 23 highly mobile vertebrae (spine-bones), and is worked by extra-strong muscles. Dogs use their tails to communicate (see page 78), but tails are also important for balance, and help stabilise a dog when it is running quickly. Dogs from icy Arctic regions, such as Spitzes or Huskies, use their thick bushy tails to insulate and protect their eyes, nose and mouth while sleeping in freezing weather.

"

In times of joy, all of us wished we possessed a tail we could wag.

Poet W. H. Auden (1907–1973)

"

Chapter Four

BARK WORSE THAN BITE?

In June 2012, on the beach at San Diego, California, over 50 dogs assembled to take part in – yes, you've guessed! – the 7th annual Dog Surfing Championships. Need to know more? Well, dogs ride the waves alone, in pairs and groups, or accompanied by their owners. Each dog is scored on its confidence on the water, the quality and length of its ride and also for its appearance. Some entrants compete in fancy dress – and the profits go to charity. From its home in Canton, Georgia, a dog called Norman has appeared on YouTube, riding a child's scooter. In Brighton, UK, there is a dog that goes skateboarding.

It seems that dogs will do almost anything that humans can. Why? Because dogs are watchers, listeners, learners, followers. They just love to join in!

How do dogs know what to do? Experts in dog behaviour think that dogs can understand about as much as a human two-year-old. (An old, sexist, Scottish saying adds: 'A collie has the mind of a man and the ways of a woman.') The experts also tell us that about 80 per cent of a dog's behaviour is governed by instinct, but that the remaining 20 per cent is learned from its companions and surroundings.

Dogs are inquisitive. They love to investigate and explore. And they like to roam, seeking food and new experiences. Dogs are also highly social. They enjoy the company of other dogs, but are also capable of forming strong bonds with humans, and learning from them. Many dogs become particularly attached to one person or family.

Dogs use several different forms of communication to establish and maintain links with their human (or canine) companions:

• **Scents:** Urine, faeces and secretions from glands near the tail all send chemical messages for other dogs to read. In return, dogs receive a constant stream of scent-messages from other dogs through their noses. An un-neutered male dog can smell a bitch in season up to 6 miles (9.6 km) away. In reply, he may leave his own calling cards (little drops of urine) up to 80 times in four hours. And every time a dog wags its tail, it is spreading a fine mist of smelly molecules all around.

• **Sounds:** Barking, growling, whining, moaning. Howling is used to communicate with other members of a dog's social group; whimpering to attract the attention of humans.

• **Special postures and gestures:** For example, when ready to attack, a dog will lean forward, weight on its front paws; when two strange dogs meet, they cautiously circle each other, sniffing nose to tail.

• **Body language:** Dogs use their ears, eyes, mouths, teeth, hair, legs and tails to send strong visual messages.

Other dogs can decipher these signals straight away. But how well can you read your dog?

Come and play!

For dogs, just like young children, play is practice for real life. As they play, dogs rehearse the moves they might one day need to make, build up their strength, and improve their skills.

Until very recently, real life for dogs involved fierce and potentially dangerous actions: fighting, growling, baring fangs. How could dogs invite others to practise these, without running the risk of being misunderstood and ending up in a fight?

For most dogs, the answer was (and still is) simple: they make a special gesture, known as the 'play bow'. They crouch down on their front legs, but keep their back legs standing. They wag their tail gently, and may bark in a friendly, unthreatening way.

I see what you mean...

Get close up and personal with your nearest friendly canine, and you will observe a wide range of movements and expressions. All have evolved to signal the dog's state of mind, and its intentions:

Eyes

- Eyes open normally = alert, playful

- Eyes wide open = excited, confident, friendly

- Eyes wide open, watchful = on guard

- Eyes wide open, following movements = chasing

- Eyes slightly narrowed = anxious

- Eyes narrowed, head turned away = fearful, avoiding conflict

- Eyes narrowed, 'whale eye' (white showing) = submissive, ready to run away

- Eyes wide open, whale eye = stressed

- Eyes narrowed, staring and glaring = aggressive – watch out!

Ears

- Ears pricked up, facing forward, relaxed = playful

- Ears pricked up, forward, perky = excited, chasing, on guard

- Ears pricked up, turned to catch sound = alert, chasing

- Ears pricked up, standing tall = dominant

- Ears pushed forward, stiffly = aggressive

- Ears flat against head = aggression or fear (depending on body posture, mouth and teeth)

- Ears tilted backwards = anxious, submissive, ready to run away

Mouth

- Mouth open, teeth 'smiling' (relaxed) = friendly

- Mouth open, teeth part-covered = playful

- Mouth open, teeth visible, panting = excited, chasing

- Mouth closed or slightly open, no teeth showing = alert

- Snarling, growling, fangs bared = aggressive

- Snarling, snapping teeth = on guard

- Lips 'grinning' (tight and tense) = anxious, submissive

- Teeth bared, drooling = fearful, ready to run away

Posture

- Posture alert, weight balanced on four paws = happy, normal

- Posture tense, leaning forwards, hackles (hair on back of neck) raised = aggression

- Posture tense, standing tall = guarding

- Posture stiff, body low, ready to spring = chasing

- Posture tense, back lowered, shivering = anxious, fearful, ready to run away

- Standing still or wriggling rear end = friendly

- Wriggling, bouncing, fast pacing = excited

- Play bow, bouncing, jumping, circling = playful

- On back, belly up, front paw raised = submission

- Licking nose = peaceful gesture, reducing stress

- Turning head away = avoiding conflict

- Turning back on = avoiding conflict

- Trapped in corner = BEWARE. An angry or frightened dog may attack first, think later. Or not think at all.

Tail

- Tail up, wagging = alert, friendly, excited

- Tail wagging wildly = playful

- Tail straight out behind, fairly low = chasing

- Tail straight or raised, perhaps fluffed up = aggression

- Tail stiff, straight behind = guarding

- Tail partly down = anxious

- Tail between legs = fear, submission, ready to run away

Bark worse than bite?

That rather depends on whether you live next door to an unhappy dog that BARKS, BARKS, BARKS all day and most of the night. Excessive dog barking can be a problem for humans – and suggests that the dog has problems, as well. But normal dogs bark in moderation, and for several different reasons.

A dog may bark because:

• it is lonely and wants company. Dogs have evolved surrounded by other wolves or dogs, and by humans. They prefer company to solitude.

• it is bored. It may lack company or may belong to a breed, such as Border Collie, that has a strong work instinct and likes to keep busy.

• it wants attention. If its owner can't see it, or doesn't understand dog body language, it needs to communicate somehow.

• it is excited or enjoying a game. So it's telling the world!

• it is doing its job. Watchdogs bark to warn their owners when strangers are approaching.

• it is frustrated, for example, trying to pick up a ball that has rolled into an inaccessible corner.

• it is in danger, trapped or afraid. It's calling for help.

Each dog has its own individual voice, but here is a general guide to what Fluffy or Fido might be saying:

• Yap, short bark, occasional whimper = friendly, excited

• Excited bark, gentle growl = playful

• Low whine, yelp, growl = fearful

• Low whine and alarm bark = alert, guarding

• Low bark, snarl, growl = guarding

• Snarl, growl, loud bark = aggressive

• Growls and grunts = dominant

• Silence = relaxed, happy

Howling – no, biting – at the moon

Folktales from many parts of the world claim that dogs are more dangerous when the moon is full. In 2000, doctors in Australia and the UK decided to test this theory by looking at statistics recording the number of people treated in hospital for dog bites. They found, bizarrely, that British dogs did bite more people when the moon is full, but that Australian dogs did not. A mystery!

Full moon or not, the total number of people injured or killed by dog bites has increased in recent years. It's a large number. In the USA, for example, about 4.7 million people are bitten every year, almost one million of them quite badly. About 25 per year, mostly children, die from their injuries. Three out of every four bites are from the pets of family or friends; around half take place on the dog-owner's property. But a few dog attacks are alarmingly different: in 2004, a pack of 200 stray dogs terrorised a small town in Albania, injuring nine people.

In praise of a well-behaved dog

…This dog hath so himself subdued
That hunger cannot make him rude,
And his behaviour does confess
True courage dwells with
  gentleness…

Katherine Philips (1632–1664),
The Irish Greyhound

The dominance debate

In the late 20th century, some scientists and professional dog trainers explained 'bad' dog behaviour, such as disobedience or aggression, by describing it as 'dominant'. They based their theories on studies of wolves, who lived in packs with a strong leader. Wolf leaders kept control over weaker pack members by fighting them, or threatening to fight. The dog trainers told owners that they must establish dominance over their pets, just like the wolves. They must become 'top dog' in their own households, and expect their pets to feel submissive to them. That way, their dogs would behave!

Many dog-owners found the trainers' tips and techniques helpful when dealing with young or problem dogs. But since around the year 2000, a growing number of scientists have challenged the whole theory of dog dominance. They say that earlier studies of wolves were based on packs of captive wolves, 'collected' from various places then sent to live in groups in an unnatural way. These stranger wolves had to 'fight it out' to find a way of living together.

More recent studies show that genuinely wild wolves live in groups based on biological families. While the pups are young and learning, their parents tell them what to do. When the parent wolves become old or die, the next generation takes over as leaders. There is no constant struggle for 'dominance', and much less fighting.

66

Animals, whom we have
made our slaves, we do not
like to consider our equal.

Charles Darwin, *Notebook B*, 1837–1838

99

CHAPTER FIVE

MAN'S BEST FRIEND

Ancient Greek soldier and statesman Alcibiades (lived around 450–404 BC) was brave, bold, brilliant, handsome and, just possibly, a psychopath. He liked to outrage and offend. One day, he chopped the tail off a dog and led it through the streets of Athens. The citizens were shocked – not at the ill-treatment of the dog, but at the disrespect shown to the law. Dogs, traditionally seen as unclean animals in the eastern Mediterranean region (see page 89), were not allowed in their city.

Over 2,000 years later, in 1698, a Dorset farmer recorded in his diary that his old and presumably worn-out dog had been killed. Matter-of-factly, he added 'and baked for his grease, of which he yielded 11 lbs [5 kg].'

Quoted in Keith Thomas, *Man and the Natural World*, 1984

Today, publicly mistreating an animal would be political suicide for any government leader, and we would not dream of putting our dead pets in the oven to extract a useful salve and lubricant from their corpses. Yet Alcibiades (for all his faults) was not intentionally being cruel, and the Dorset farmer was not deliberately being heartless. So what was going on?

Alcibiades was using the poor tail-less dog to make the citizens of Athens look foolish, and to stop them criticising his own political crimes and ambitions. He boasted to his friends that the citizens would make a fuss over anything new and strange – even a dog without a tail – and, for a while, forget all about important things such as politics.

If it looks like a dog...

The Greeks were fascinated by the natural world, and were keen to examine and classify (describe and sort into sets) all kinds of living things, including dogs. They had no knowledge of evolution or prehistoric creatures, of genetics or DNA. So they described creatures in the way that seemed most logical to them: how each one was structured, where it lived, and how it reproduced.

By observing various living things and comparing them with men and women, Greek scientists could also evaluate humanity's relationship to other creatures. They considered humans to be greater than 'brute' beasts, because only humans could use reason.

By cutting off his poor dog's tail, Alcibaides had destroyed its 'dogginess': its proper, natural, shape and beauty. This was wrong, as well as surprising. However, compared with humans, a dog's suffering did not really matter. It was a lesser creature; an animal.

Don't waste it

Like Alcibiades, the Dorset farmer was also using his dog. If challenged about his behaviour, he might well have quoted a saying popular among poor country people: 'Waste not, want not!' He had probably used his dog all its life, as a watchdog or guard dog, or perhaps for herding sheep and cattle. We have no evidence that he treated it unkindly while it was alive; it had a name ('Quon'), which suggests that he saw it as an individual creature. It was big; to obtain '11 lb grease' you might need a well-covered dog weighing 40 lb (18 kg) or more. It had lived to a good old age. So it seems to have been well looked after, housed and fed. But its dead body, compared with a human's, was not important.

'Necessary' dogs

Although they lived at different times and in different civilisations, the Dorset farmer and Alcibiades would almost certainly have agreed on one point: that known, named, domesticated dogs were necessary. Humans needed them; without dogs, life would be very difficult. Until around 1700 or even later, most people saw dogs as 'living tools': creatures that existed to help humans.

Hated and feared

Stories from ancient Egypt and the Hebrew Bible describe similar scenes: a wife deceives her husband or his people; a wicked man is caught; an evil ruler is overthrown. As a punishment, they are all 'thrown to the dogs' – the packs of wild or feral dogs that roamed the streets of many ancient towns and cities after dark. The dogs were hated and feared – not least because their victims' bodies would have been pulled apart by hungry jaws, and eaten.

Dogs like these were always ravenous, usually dirty, and liable to spread very dangerous diseases. They belonged to no-one, and were best left alone. They were the lowest of the low; man's enemies, not his friends.

Workaday world

Unlike the dangerous, disease-ridden street dogs, domestic dogs could be trained to carry out all kinds of useful duties. In ancient Egypt, desert police used dogs to track runaway criminals. Most ordinary working dogs were probably mongrels, but, for different tasks, the Greeks and Romans developed three special kinds of dogs, and imported a fourth:

• **Laconians:** fast hunting dogs that tracked their prey by scent. Greek writer Xenophon said that hounds should 'give chase eagerly without resting and with much barking and noise...They should chase swiftly and skilfully, rushing along after the hare in a pack, calling and yelping...again and again.'

• **Vertragi:** By Roman times, the best hunting dogs came from the British Isles. They were tall, slim, fine-boned and short-coated: 'swifter than thought or a winged bird'. They tracked prey by sight.

Come, Spot! Here, Barker!

An ancient Greek myth tells a terrible story. Actaeon, a young hero was hunting in the forest. By chance, he caught sight of Artemis, goddess of hunting and the moon, bathing naked in a forest pool. Outraged, she turned him into a stag and his own hounds chased and devoured him. A retelling of this myth by the Roman poet Ovid (died AD 18) tells us the names of all Actaeon's hounds; he had 50(!). Here are just some – we might still recognise them as names for dogs today:

Argiodus (White Fang)
Asbolos (Soot)
Canache (Gnasher)
Harpalos (Grasper)
Hylactor (Barker)
Lachne (Shaggy)
Sticte (Spot)

• **Molossians:** large, heavy, fierce guard dogs. Greek poet Hesiod (lived around 700 BC) advised: 'Make much of your sharp-toothed dog; do not stint his food, lest the man who sleeps by day steal your possessions.' Watchdogs also feature in *Cave Canem* (Beware of the Dog) mosaics from Roman city houses. Ideally, a guard dog had a big head, droopy ears, thickset shoulders and neck, large paws, a thick tail, and a deep, loud bark.

The Romans also bred mastiff-type dogs to take part in contests against wild beasts and gladiators in the arena, and to fight alongside their masters in battle.

• **Cretans:** working dogs, probably bred from a fast, sleek hound crossed with a heavy watchdog. The favourite dog of many Greek and Roman farmers. Brave and eager, they went hunting and guarded homes and livestock.

Special duties

A few Greek and Roman dogs were also trained for unusual duties. For example, in Greece, doctor and teacher Hippocrates used dogs to tell whether an apparently lifeless body was dead or still just breathing. (The dogs either barked, or stayed silent). In Rome, some dogs won fame as entertainers:

In the first century AD, Roman writer Plutarch described a talented (and trusting) dog that belonged to an actor. It played several different roles on stage. In one, it had to pretend that it had been fatally poisoned. On its owner's command, it ate a piece of bread smeared with drugs that caused drowsiness. It collapsed – dramatically – and lay still, hardly breathing. By the end of the play, the effect of the drugs wore off and the dog regained consciousness. It staggered across the stage to receive a 'thank you' pat from its owner, 'not without the joy and good content of Caesar and all the other beholders'.*

*John Ashton, *Curious Creatures in Zoology*, 1890

Humans rule, OK?

After the Roman empire weakened, around AD 400, the Christian Church became the most powerful and influential organisation in Europe. Following Biblical tradition, Church leaders taught that God had created animals, including dogs, to be the obedient servants of humanity. All living creatures could be used, and if need be, killed, to benefit people:

> And let them [humanity] have dominion [rule] over the fish of the sea, and over the fowl of the air, and over the cattle, and over all the earth, and over every creeping thing that creepeth upon the earth…
>
> Genesis, Chapter 1, verse 26

For the next thousand years and more, some humans placed very heavy demands on their animals. Dogs were expected to fight to the death to defend their owners' lives and property, or to bait (attack and torment) huge and savage bears for sport. Furious bulls were baited by dogs as well; people thought that their meat was inedible, otherwise. Hunting dogs might be killed by dangerous prey, such as stags or wild boar. Dog fights were popular entertainment. Working dogs might spend most of their time chained up, or turning a waterwheel or a roasting spit over a fire. Some might stagger under heavy loads. Owners thought nothing of killing unwanted dogs and puppies. And we have read about puppy-water (page 50)…

Like most other animals, dogs were seen as 'brute' beasts, savage and sinful by nature. Wandering dogs were driven away by beating and stoning. So were abandoned dogs and strays. Dogs caught chasing wild game or killing sheep might be cruelly punished, even hanged like human criminals. If medieval writers are to be believed, at the end of tough, hard-working lives, many dogs were simply thrown away.

Nothing wittier than a hound

Franciscan friar Bartholomew the Englishman describes a dog's life – and death – around 1250:

Nothing is more busy and wittier than a hound, for he hath more wit [intelligence] than other beasts. And hounds know their own names, and love their masters, and defend the houses of their masters, and put themselves wilfully in peril of death for their masters, and run to take prey for their masters, and forsake not the dead bodies of their masters. We have known that hounds fought for their lords against thieves, and were sore wounded, and that they kept away beasts and fowls from their masters' bodies dead…

… and at the last [at the end of his life] the hound is violently drawn out of the dunghill with a rope or with a whip bound about his neck, and is drowned in the river, or in some other water, and so he endeth his wretched life. And his skin is not taken off, nor his flesh is not eaten or buried, but left finally to flies, and to other divers [various] worms.

Class conscious

In 1570, English doctor, college principal and keen student of animal life Dr John Caius published a book, *De Canibus Britannicis* (translated in 1576 as *On British Dogges*). It described in remarkable detail the different types of dogs commonly kept in Britain, and what kind of person they belonged to. Unlike the ancient Greeks and Romans, Dr Caius did not identify dogs by their shape or size, as part of the natural world. And, although devoutly Christian, he did not call them brutish or sinful. Instead, he described each different kind of dog according to the work they did for humans – and then divided this work, and the dogs, into three different classes.

He called some dogs 'gentle' (high-class) because they worked for high-ranking people. These top dogs took part in high-status activities such as hunting, or else lived lives of ease and privilege as pets. All other British dogs were low-ranking workers, like their owners. Some 'rustic' (peasant) dogs were trusty and dutiful. Other, worse, dogs were sullen, suspicious, 'degenerate'.

• **Well-bred, gentle dogs**

Hunting dogs: Terrier, Harrier, Bloodhound, Gaze-hound, Greyhound, Leviter (Leash-hound) or Bloodhound, Tumbler

Retrievers: Spaniel, Setter, Water-Spaniel or Finder

Pets: Spaniel-Gentle or Comforter

• **Rural, rough, peasant dogs**

Shepherd's dog, Bandedog or Mastiff (includes: Watchdog, Messenger, Butcher's dog/Cattle dog, Water-drawer (turns wheel to lift water from wells), Defender, and Tinker's Cur (carries a tinker's tools and equipment, and guards him).

• **Degenerate dogs**

Warning dog, Turnspit dog (walks in wheel to turn spit-roast over fire), Dancer (does tricks to 'move men to laughter for a little lucre').

Dr Caius expected that most worker dogs would spend their lives as necessary servants to humans. Some would be well-treated, others would suffer. A few (we don't know how many) might become the valued companions of the men and women who owned them. But they remained animals, living tools – not equals, not friends.

Ay, in the catalogue ye go for men;
As hounds, and greyhounds, mongrels, spaniels, curs,
Shoughs, water-rugs, and demi-wolves, are 'clept
All by the name of dogs: the valued file
Distinguishes the swift, the slow, the subtle,
The housekeeper, the hunter, every one
According to the gift which bounteous nature
Hath in him closed.

William Shakespeare, *Macbeth*, act 3, scene 1

clept = called, named
file = rank, ability, skill
closed = enclosed, placed, put

66

I am 'a dog who sleeps in the tent, a hound of the bed, whom his mistress loves…'

An Egyptian royal official describes his devotion to the Pharaoh by likening himself to a pet dog, around 1500 BC.

99

CHAPTER SIX

HIS FAITHFUL DOG SHALL BEAR HIM COMPANY

Poet Alexander Pope (1688–1744)

Roman army commander Julius Caesar (100–44 BC) was a very busy man. As well as invading Britain, conquering Gaul (France), escaping from pirates, writing a joke-book and (so his enemies said) plotting to take over the government, he also found time to complain that the women of Rome were paying too much attention to their pet dogs, and not enough to their children.

We don't know whether Caesar had a genuine cause for concern. The same complaint was still being made 1,500 years later, about rich women in Tudor England; maybe the (male) complainants were jealous. But Caesar's remark tells us that not everyone in the ancient world treated dogs just as 'necessary' workers. To a fortunate few – the rich, the powerful – dogs were cherished pets. These high-status people had the money, the time (whatever Caesar said), the freedom and the inclination to love and care for their dogs, and to enjoy expensive, exclusive sports that relied on dogs, such as hunting.

Pharaoh's favourites

Evidence of beloved pet dogs survives from as early as 1500 BC in ancient Egypt. There, wall-paintings and carved memorial stones from tombs show dogs sitting patiently under their rich owners' chairs. The dogs seem to have been produced by careful breeding; they look rather like the Saluki today. They wear decorated collars, and have descriptive names, such as 'Ebony', 'Antelope' and 'The Brave One'. A few dogs even have tombs of their own. Their owners paid for their bodies to be made into mummies, hoping that their dogs' faithful spirits would live for ever.

From ancient Greece, the *Odyssey* (composed using earlier stories around 800 BC) tells us that Odysseus's old dog Argos had gone hunting with his master, but was also 'fed from his master's table, and kept for show'. Greek painted vases picture pet dogs from wealthy families, going for walks on leads with their masters, or playing at home with women and children.

Unlike the huge hunting dog Argos, these household pets were very small, creamy-white, and fluffy. Greeks and Romans called them 'dogs from the island of Malta'; modern Maltese Terriers are very similar. These little dogs could sit on their owner's laps or be hidden in the folds of long, loose clothing and carried around. Critics of Roman emperor Claudius (died AD 54) accused him of doing this – a way of saying that he was weak, like a woman.

But other Greek and Roman men were also fond of their little lapdogs. One wealthy Roman, Publius, even paid for painters to make a portrait of his pet, so that he would have a lasting reminder of her beauty. Pet dogs are shown on several tombstones; there are also Roman memorial inscriptions, like this one from Italy:

My eyes are wet with tears, our dear little dog…Patricius (Noble)… you were so clever and knowing, almost like a human.

Prize possessions

The Celts and Vikings kept hunting dogs, too. They were prize posessions, worth as much as horse, and greatly admired. Warrior-hero Finn McCooll's dog, Bran, was described as 'a ferocious, small-headed, white-breasted, sleek-haunched hound; having the eyes of a dragon, the claws of a wolf, the vigour of a lion, and the venom of a serpent'. Viking goddess Frigga, guardian of marriage, was said to ride in a chariot pulled by dogs famous for trust and faithfulness.

Faithful friends

Elsewhere in medieval Europe, Christian Church leaders frowned on excessive displays of affection towards 'brute' and 'unclean' or 'sinful' animals. According to Church law, cats were the only pets allowed in monasteries, for pest-control. But the 'no pets' rule was often ignored:

A 'tender heart'

Geoffrey Chaucer (died 1400) describes a vain, sentimental prioress (head of a community of nuns):

She was so charitable and so piteous [full of pity],
She would weep if that she saw a mouse
Caught in a trap, if it were dead or bled.
Of small hounds had she, that she fed
With roasted flesh, and milk, and wastel bread
 [fine white bread],
But sore she wept if one of them were dead,
Or if men smote [hit] it with a yarde smart
 [painful big stick]:
And all was conscience and tender heart.

Canterbury Tales, General Prologue

However, soon after Chaucer was writing, artists working for the Church were using lapdogs as symbols of faithfulness and loyalty, especially in marriage. A magnificent stained-glass window in Cologne, Germany, created around 1500, shows a respectable married couple in a richly covered double bed. Curled up at their feet is a little lapdog, sleeping peacefully. The moral message is clear: this is the correct, happy, untroubled way to behave.

Gentlemen, gentle dogs

By the sixteenth and seventeeth centuries, it seemed as if almost everyone at royal courts throughout Europe was a dog lover. Dogs were the height of fashion, and an English proverb declared: 'He cannot be a gentleman that loveth not a dog.' But only two kinds of dogs were considered suitable as pets. These were the breeds described by Dr Caius as 'gentle' (page 98): hunting dogs and lapdogs. Many of these pets were very well treated. For hounds, spacious kennels were built at royal palaces and nobles' stately homes. Grooms slept there too; conditions were often cleaner and more comfortable than in poor cottages. Lapdogs slept, as we saw at Cologne, on their owners' beds. This was not without problems. In 1665, London diary-writer Samuel Pepys reported that his close friend Mrs Penington was 'mightily troubled' because her pet dog was ill. The lady took the sick dog to bed with her – with extremely messy consequences.

Queen shoots dog

In spite of all the care lavished upon them, rich peoples' pets sometimes suffered because of their owners' misfortunes – or miscalculation. We can hardly imagine the feelings of the little black-and-white spaniel belonging to Mary Queen of Scots when the executioner cut off its mistress's head. The dog bravely stayed in place underneath the dead queen's robes – and gave onlookers a terrible fright, by making the skirts heave and shuffle. The dog died 5 days later – from a broken heart, people said.

Mary's son, King James VI of Scotland and I of England, was also a famous dog-fancier; critics said that he loved his pets more than his people. Alas, one of James's favourite hounds was accidentally mistaken for a deer and shot dead – by his wife, Queen Anne.

'Instrumentes of folly'

At the same time as wealthy people were pampering their pets, the poor were hungry and sometimes starving. Extravagant spending on dogs was therefore roundly criticised, by priests and poor protesters. Critics also felt that the love shown by ladies to their dogs was immodest and extreme. Pets turned their owners' minds away from serious, suitable topics of study; they wasted time. Even dog-lover Dr Caius complained:

> These dogges are litle, pretty, proper, and fyne, and sought for to satisfie the delicatenesse of daintie dames, and wanton [immoral] womens wills, instrumentes of folly for them to play and dally withall, to tryfle away the treasure of time, to withdraw their mindes from more commendable exercises, and to content their corrupted concupiscences [appetites] with vaine disport [unworthy pleasures]…

On British Dogges, 1570

Lords of creation?

But the fact that 'wanton women' liked to lull pet dogs 'in theyr lappes...[and]...kysse them with their lippes' was important. In a messy, emotional kind of way, it echoed the concerns of the top European philosophers. As they rediscovered the writings of ancient Greek and Roman scientists after around 1450, philosophers began to look at all living creatures, including human beings, in a new way. They asked, did men and women really have God-given dominion over creation? Were not animals, including dogs, equally fascinating examples of the wonder of the natural world?

Yes, they were, but that did not stop dog-lovers like Pepys happily going to watch one of the first ever experiments in blood transfusion, in 1665. Blood was taken from a mastiff and transferred into the veins of a spaniel. The spaniel survived, but the mastiff bled to death. No-one minded too much. It was only a working dog.

Witchcraft!

In spite of changing ideas, even royal dogs were not always safe from very old superstitions. In Pepys's day, people still believed in witches, and claimed that small pet animals, usually cats but sometimes dogs, were witches' 'familars' (tame evil spirits). English army leader Prince Rupert (1619–1682) owned a rare white poodle named Boye that always rode with him, perched on his horse. His enemies claimed that Boye was a familiar, or even a witch in disguise, and gave Rupert an unfair advantage in battle. The dog was killed during the fighting at Marston Moor in 1644, during the English Civil War. It was the first battle in England that Prince Rupert did not win.

Good or bad?

Thoughtful people were well aware of this double-think towards dogs. On the one hand, dogs were cherished pets, on the other, they were either unimportant workers, or, even worse, witches. Poet and politician Sir John

Davies (1569–1626) summed up these contrasting attitudes in verses written to one of his friends:

> Thou say'st thou art as weary as a dog,
> As angry, sick, and hungry as a dog,
> As dull and melancholy as a dog,
> As lazy, sleepy, idle as a dog.
> But why dost thou compare thee to a dog
> In that for which all men despise a dog?
> I will compare thee better to a dog;
> Thou art as fair and comely as a dog,
> Thou art as true and honest as a dog,
> Thou art as kind and liberal as a dog,
> Thou art as wise and valiant as a dog…

Dog lover or dog hater, the choice was up to the individual. And the time was soon approaching when some leading thinkers would be asking: 'Don't dogs have feelings and preferences, too?' You can read more about this in Chapter 8.

"

Men with heads of dogs, who clothe themselves in the skins of wild beasts. Instead of speaking, they bark. Furnished with claws, they live by hunting, and catching birds.

From a description of India by the ancient Greek historian and geographer Ctesias, who lived around 400 BC

"

CHAPTER SEVEN

WORTHY OF WONDER

Ancient Greek philosopher Plato
(427–347 BC), about dogs

O n 4 August 1577, 'A Straunge and Terrible Wunder' was said to have taken place in the parish church of Bungay, Suffolk (eastern England):

there appeared in a most horrible similitude and likenesse to the congregation...a dog...of a black colour; at the site [sight] whereof, togither with the fearful flashes of fire which were then seene, moved such admiration [wonder] in the minds of the assemblie, that they thought doomesday was already come. This black dog, or the divil in such a likenesse...passed betweene two persons, as they were kneeling upon their knees, and occupied in prayer...,wrung [twisted] the necks of them bothe at one instant clene [sharply] backward...[and]...they strangely died.

Source:

http://www.blackdoginstitute.org.au/docs/Michael.pdf

Yes! It was yet another hell-hound, this time the Devil himself, come to frighten the wits out of peaceful people. For over two thousand years, in Europe, North Africa and the Middle East, dogs, as described in myths, legends, religious texts and popular beliefs, had been closely linked to the Land of the Dead.

By nature, dogs are crepuscular: they become most active in the half-light of dawn and at dusk, after sunset. Perhaps this is why they were so often linked with death and darkness. And they were scavengers, who could sniff out carrion...

A bloody end

In ancient Egypt, dog-headed or jackal-headed Anubis was the god of death and of graveyards. In Greek and Roman myths, three-headed dog Cerberus guarded the entrance to the Underworld; witch-goddess Hecate was sometimes portrayed with a dog's head, and worshipped at midnight. Dogs also featured in Greek and Roman religious sacrifices.

Picture the scene. Place? Ancient Rome. Date? 15 February, the festival of Lupercalia. Purpose? To celebrate the birth of the city of Rome and to bring fertility. Action? First, two goats and a dog were killed, as sacrifices to the gods. Using the same knife, their blood was daubed on the foreheads of two youths from high-ranking families. The sacrificed animals were washed in milk, then skinned. Their skins were cut into strips, and given to the young men. Stark naked, the youths ran around, whipping everyone they met with bloody strips of skin. Women who hoped to get pregnant made sure that they stood at the front of the crowd.

Greek dog sacrifices were rather more decorous but, for the dogs, just as lethal. At the festival of Arnis (also called *kunophontis* – dog-killing day), stray dogs were rounded up and sacrificed in memory of Linus, love-child of a human princess and the god Apollo. Linus had been left to die on a mountainside and ripped to pieces by wild dogs. As punishment to the princess and her people, Apollo sent an evil spirit that killed local children.

An awful warning

In Celtic myths, there was the horrid black Moddey Dhoo, a giant black dog from the Isle of Man, and the white-coated, red-eared Hounds of Annwn. They met young Welsh prince Pwyll in the forest – and led him out of this world to meet their master, the king of the Underworld. Ever after, a hound's baying was said to be a warning of death. Later folktales from many parts of Europe (and the USA) describe the same hounds – often known as the Wild Hunt – racing across the sky, this time led by the Lord of Death-in-Battle. It was very, very bad luck to see them.

In real life, Celtic dogs were often buried in deep pools and at the bottom of disused wells – to the Celts, both were entrances to the Underworld. Perhaps they were put there to guard the land of the living against intruders, or to keep all the horrors of the land of the dead safely shut away.

Ghostly hounds

Coming closer to our own day and age, vengeful ghosts were often portrayed as dogs. For centuries, Newgate prison in London was said to be haunted by the spirit of a scholar who had dabbled in witchcraft. He was arrested and taken there in 1596, and – so the lurid story goes – killed and eaten by the starving prisoners. Soon afterwards, a strange black dog appeared. The cannibal prisoners overpowered their guards and escaped, but the ghost-dog haunted them for the rest of their lives.

Even more recently, hell-hounds feature in one of the world's best-loved detective stories, Sir Arthur Conan Doyle's *The Hound of the Baskervilles*, published in 1902:

> A hound it was, an enormous coal-black hound, but not such a hound as mortal eyes have ever seen. Fire burst from its open mouth, its eyes glowed with a smouldering glare, its muzzle and hackles and dewlap were outlined in flickering flame. Never in the delirious dream of a disordered brain could anything more savage, more appalling, more hellish be conceived than that dark form and savage face which broke upon us out of the wall of the fog.

Shepherds of souls

On the other hand, some supernatural dogs were friendly, helpful creatures. Statues of Celtic mother-goddesses often show them accompanied by little dogs, and dogs also seem to have been kept – or sacrificed – at Celtic healing sanctuaries. The story of famous Celtic hero CuChulainn tells how, as Setanta, a magic child with supernatural strength, he killed a prized guard-dog. To make amends, Setanta changed his name (CuChullain means 'the Hound of Cullen') and agreed to take the dog's place for a while.

Viking tombstones show heroes arriving at Valhalla, home of the glorious dead, to find their favourite dogs waiting to welcome them. A comforting thought! Viking warriors were often buried with dogs to guide them through the dangers of death to a happy resting place. However, one Viking saga suggests that dogs were not always seen in such a positive light:

Viking King Eystein was a tough warrior and a harsh ruler. After winning many battles and conquering vast lands, he made his son king of Norway. The Norwegian people were not happy about this, and Eystein's son was murdered. Eystein was furious, and took a terrible revenge, attacking and devastating his son's former kingdom. At last, after the Norwegians had been forced to admit defeat, Eystein offered them a mocking choice of new ruler: would they rather have his servant as their next king, or a dog?

The Norwegians chose the dog. (They thought it would be easier to ignore than the servant.) It was called Saur (excrement), which tells us what Eystein thought of the Norwegians, and of dogs. In fact, the dog was said to be 'as wise as three men'. It wore a gold-and-silver collar, and was carried around on cushions by palace servants.

As a cruel but effective trick, the Norwegians arranged for the palace cattle-barns to be attacked by wild wolves. The king-dog rushed to defend his livestock, and was killed.

All round the world

The idea of dogs as psychopomps (guides of dead souls) appears in myths worldwide, from Central America, where Maya dogs escorted the dead across a perilous lake, to Hindu Nepal, where dogs were said to stand at the gates of heaven as well as hell. Nepali dogs are still honoured at the annual Tihar festival, where they are garlanded with flowers.

Seven sleepers – but no angels

There are contrasting Islamic traditions about dogs. The holy Qur'an encourages respect for all of God's creation, including dogs, and tells the story of the Seven Sleepers. These were young people living under ancient Roman rule – later traditions say they were from Ephesus, now in Turkey, but this is not certain. They refused to give up their faith in the One God and chose instead to be killed as martyrs, by being walled up in a cave. Their dog went with them.

At the same time, some Hadith (traditional accounts of the good example set by the Prophet Muhammad) say that angels will not enter a house where a dog is present. They urge Muslims not to own dogs as pets, but only to keep them for 'necessary' reasons, such as herding livestock or guarding houses. Hunting dogs should be set to work 'in the name of God', otherwise their prey will be unclean. Black dogs are seen (as in Christian traditions) as signs of the devil. However, not all Hadith are accepted as equally valid by different groups within Islam.

The sign of fidelity

In China, the dog, Gou (fidelity), is one of the twelve signs of the traditional calendar. People born in the Year of the Dog are said to be honest, reliable, responsible, compassionate, curious, anxious, pessimistic and sometimes rather overwhelming.

Pekingese dogs, bred in China since the Han dynasty (206 BC–AD 220), were considered sacred; only the royal family and favoured courtiers could own them. Anyone who stole a Pekingese was executed, and the dogs themselves were killed whenever an emperor died, to go with their master into the next world.

In Tibet, Lhasa Apso dogs were tended by Buddhist monks, and took part in temple ceremonies. They were said to symbolise lions, perpetually standing guard over the Buddha.

Dog-men, men-dogs?

Strange tales of men with dog's heads have been told since ancient Greek times (see page 112). Often, these monsters were simply ways of expressing excitement and curiosity about the exotic and unknown. But what are we to make of Christian saints who looked like dogs? Here are two to consider:

St Christopher, a giant, was said to have bravely carried Christ across a raging river. He is sometimes shown in Orthodox Christian icons (holy pictures) with the head of a dog. In medieval England, scholars added that 'his locks were extremely long, and his eyes shone as bright as the morning star, and his teeth were as sharp as a boar's tusks'.* At least three traditions are mingled here: the ancient idea of the dog as escort of souls; the Christian teaching that man's nature is beastly but can be saved through faith and good deeds; and the notion that people in far-distant lands are 'not like us'. And maybe more.

*http://oe-stchristopher.blogspot.co.uk/

Stranger still is the story of dog-saint Guinefort. It combines a folktale found around half the world with ancient healing rituals. The tale tells of a dog left to guard a child while its master goes away. A snake attacks the child; the dog bravely kills it. When the master returns, he sees the bloodstained dog and jumps to the wrong conclusion – that the dog has murdered the child. He kills the dog, but then discovers the child safe and well, with the dead snake close by.

In the 13th century, scandalised Christian friars found French peasants praying at Guinefort's tomb, and asking him (or it) to cure their sick children. Peasant mothers hung baby-clothes on bushes close to the tomb, passed their babies to and fro between the trunks of ancient trees. They lit candles, and then left the babies naked on the ground for the saint to cure – or kill. The mothers did not know this, but the trees were probably the remains of a Celtic sacred grove; 'clootie wells' (cloth-offerings) were found in many Celtic countries. And, as we have seen, Celtic people believed that dogs had powers of healing.

A medieval pun – and a medieval dream

The Christian friars who found Guinefort's tomb were nicknamed the 'hounds of God', because they were zealous – and because they belonged to the brotherhood founded by St Dominic (1170–1221). In Latin, the language of the Church, a follower of St Dominic is a *Dominicanus*. It sounds very similar to *Domini canes*, which means 'the dogs of the Lord'.

After St Dominic won fame and praise, stories began to be told about how, when pregnant, his mother had had a dream. In it, a dog leapt from her womb, declaring that it was going to set the world on fire.

"

A dog reflects the family life. Whoever saw a frisky dog in a gloomy family, or a sad dog in a happy one? Snarling people have snarling dogs, dangerous people have dangerous ones.

Detective Sherlock Holmes, in Sir Arthur Conan Doyle's *The Case-Book of Sherlock Holmes*, 1927

"

CHAPTER EIGHT

LOVE ME, LOVE MY DOG

Monarchs don't often feel the need to advertise in the 'Lost and Found' columns of national newspapers, but in 1660, King Charles II of England did just that:

We must call upon you again for a Black Dog between a greyhound and a spaniel, no white about him, onely a streak on his brest, and his tayl a little bobbed. It is His Majesties own Dog, and doubtless was stoln, for the dog was not born nor bred in England, and would never forsake His master. Whoesoever findes him may acquaint any at Whitehal for the Dog was better known at Court, than those who stole

him. Will they never leave robbing his
Majesty! Must he not keep a Dog?

Mercurius Publicus, 28 June – 5 July, 1660, quoted in
Notes and Queries, 7th Series , vol. vii, p. 26

King Charles II (ruled 1660–1685) came from
a family of dog-lovers – and is the only English
king to have a breed of dog named after
himself (King Charles Spaniel, distorted by
breeders during the 19th century, and
recreated through selective breeding as the
Cavalier King Charles Spaniel in the 20th
century). Exiled as a young man to France
and the Netherlands, Charles met other royal
families who were also passionate about dogs.
As child, Charles's cousin, King Louis XIV of
France, kept ten dogs in his rooms and
fed them with biscuits baked by the palace
pastrycook.

Charles's aunt, the 'Winter Queen' of
Bohemia, was said to prefer her pet dogs (she
had 20) to any of her children (she had 13).
Charles's sister, Princess Henrietta Anne,
dressed her lapdog in large red tassel earrings.
Charles himself was painted, aged about 7,

standing with his arm on the head of an enormous mastiff, almost as tall as he is.

Historians have suggested that pets like these provided an emotional outlet for high-ranking people. Kings, queen and courtiers were obliged to marry and have children for duty, not love, and to live almost like prisoners, surrounded by servants and bodyguards. Royal dogs also had practical uses. Before riding on horseback, young princes often practised by riding big dogs. Teams of dogs were also kept in palaces to taste portions of food, to check that a dish was not poisoned.

These royal dogs were 'gentle' – of course. But many were more than that. They came from new, rare, exotic varieties. For example, in the early sixteenth century, German Prince Henry IV of Saxony owned an elegant gazelle hound, a type of dog that originated in North Africa or the Middle East. Charles II's advertisement for his lost dog suggests that it was perhaps a crossbreed, and possibly of a type not yet well-known in Britain.

Breeding true

From as early as 4000 BC, distinct varieties of dog began to develop in different parts of the world. They included Dingoes in Australia, Chows Chows in China, Akita Inu in Japan, Basenji in Central Africa, Huskies in Siberia and Malamutes in Alaska, Salukis in the Middle East and Afghan Hounds in nearby Central Asia. (There, Mongol emperor Genghis Khan (died 1227) was reputed to own a record number of dogs: 5,000 fierce mastiffs.)

Further east, Chinese dog-keepers, working for emperors and nobles, were some of the first experimental dog-breeders. They aimed to produce miniature versions of the native local dogs, which were stocky, long- coated, with curled tails and pointed muzzles. A particularly small variety was known as a 'sleeve-dog', because it could be tucked into the long, wide sleeves of robes worn at the Chinese court.

No lists, no rules

However, at the time when Charles II's dog went missing in 1660, breeds from Asia and Africa were largely unknown in Europe, and pedigree dogs as we know them today had not been invented. People did breed dogs for specific purposes – to hunt, to guard, to herd and even to be pets. And farmers or shepherds would do their best to obtain puppies with a good local reputation for intelligence, obedience, fierceness or whatever other canine quality they needed. In 1665, diarist Samuel Pepys recorded his careful choice of mate (based on good looks) for his wife's pet spaniel. But detailed listing and checking of dog pedigrees was not widespread anywhere until the mid-19th century.

Looking and learning

Throughout the 18th century, European farmers, landowners and scholars began to take a more scientific interest in animals. They wanted to improve farming and make it more profitable; they were fascinated by news of exotic wildlife seen by sailors, traders and colonists as they travelled round the world. Artists created proud portraits of huge, prize farm animals and published exquisite studies of birds and flowers. For the first time, the 36-volume *Natural History*, compiled by leading French scientist, the Comte de Buffon (1707–1788), described the anatomy of all kinds of creatures, including dogs. Wealthy followers of sports such as horse-racing, hare-coursing and fox-hunting shared this new interest in dogs' bodies and how worked; they wanted to breed the best possible horses and hounds. In England, foxhound pedigrees were officially recorded from 1787.

In 1796, all dogs in Britain were taxed. Records show that the dog population had by then reached around 1 million: around one dog for every eight people, approximately the same proportion as today. Many of these dogs were working animals; some were foxhounds, some were pets. A few were still kept to take part in cruel sports, such as dog-fights (held in arenas known as 'pits' – hence Pit Bull Terriers). Other sporting dogs, owned by working people rather than rich or noble families, were bred to chase rabbits, to go poaching, and to race each other. Greyhound pedigrees were nationally recorded from 1882.

The final verse of the 'Ballad of Master McGrath' celebrates a famous Irish greyhound. Master McGrath won the prestigious Waterloo Cup for hare-coursing three times in its short life (1866–1873), and was invited to meet Queen Victoria.

I've known many greyhounds that filled me with pride,
In the days that are gone, but it can't be denied,
That the greatest and the bravest that the world ever saw,
Was our champion of champions, great Master McGrath.

McGrath is pronounced 'Mac-Graw'.

A new view

At the same time, attitudes towards dogs – and all other animals – were changing. Leading writers and thinkers began to ask: Did animals have feelings and maybe, even, rights? Did they not feel pain? Should they not be spared suffering?

In Germany, brilliant, austere (and difficult) philosopher Immanuel Kant (1724–1804) wrote: 'We can judge the heart of a man by his treatment of animals.' In Scotland, ploughman-poet Robert Burns celebrated the individual character and joyful exuberance of his brother's collie.

Luath (Swift), the dog in question, was not a 'living tool' but a fellow-creature:

> He was a gash and faithfu' tyke
> As ever lapt a sheugh or dyke.
> His honest, sawnsie, bawsint face
> Aye gat him friends in ilka place.
> His breast was white, his towsie back

Weel clad wi' coat o' glossy black.
His gawcie tail, wi' upward curl
Hung ower his hurdies wi' a swurl…

Robert Burns, 'The Twa Dogs', 1786

gash = wise
sheugh = ditch
dyke = wall
sawnsie = bonny
bawsint = white-striped
aye gat = always got/always found
ilka = every
towsie= tousled
weel = well
gawcie = jolly
hurdies = rear end

In 1822, the UK parliament passed Martin's Act, to ban 'the cruel and improper treatment of cattle'. The world's first animal welfare charity, the RSPCA, was founded in London in 1824. Soon after, in 1835, another UK law, Pease's Act, forbade cruelty to dogs and domestic animals. Bear-baiting and dog-fights were outlawed.

Showing off

The first organised dog shows were held towards the end of the 18th century. Huntsmen, farmers and dog-lovers met to examine and admire favourite animals and discuss how they might be bettered. Dog breeders exhibited exotic dogs from distant lands, or experimented by creating new crossbreeds, such as Jack Russells (from 1815) and Golden Retrievers (from the 1860s). The first Labradors came to Britain in the 1870s, from North America; Pekingese from China around 1860; Rottweilers (originally bear-hunters and then cattle-dogs) from Germany, in 1936.

Before long, the shows became competitions; the first Birmingham National show, accepting entries from all over the UK, was organised in 1859. Crufts dog show, now world famous, was first held in 1886.

Royal favour

As in King Charles II's day, royal patronage made some breeds very popular. During her long life, Queen Victoria (1837–1901) owned 35 Pomeranians, together with several spaniels, terriers and collies. She paid for many of her canine friends to be commemorated in paintings and statues, helping to set a sentimental new fashion for animals in art. She wrote that cruelty to animals was 'one of the worst signs of wickedness in human nature'.

Kennel Clubs

At first, there were no regulations about dog-breeding. This was not always good for dogs or dog owners; breeders might be cruel, greedy, exploitative, unscrupulous – and more – and there were many opportunities for fraud. In 1873, the UK Kennel Club was formed to keep a register of all pure-bred dogs, and to co-ordinate the activities of reputable dog breeders. The American Kennel Club was set up in 1884, soon followed by the

Kennel Club of Canada. In 1911 the Fédération Cynologique Internationale (FCI) was founded by dog-breeders in Germany, Austria, Belgium, France and the Netherlands; by the 21st century it had 86 member countries, and held a 'World Show' for dogs every year.

Today, there are over 400 known breeds of dog, although not all are recognised by all dog-breeders' associations. To be accepted as breed members, dogs have to meet detailed specifications for general appearance, character, temperament, body conformation (nose to tail), gait, coat, colour and size.

As Sherlock Holmes's comment suggested (page 126), people tend to choose dogs that somehow reflect themselves. Readers, this may be *lèse majesté*, but I always think Charles II's long curly wigs look like his favourite spaniels' ears. Today, there are websites showing dogs said to look like their owners…

Top dog breeds

Currently, 210 different breeds are recognised by the Kennel Club in the UK, and 175 by the American Kennel Club. In 2011, the Top Ten – no, the Top Thirteen – most popular dog breeds were:

UK	USA
1. Labrador Retriever	Labrador Retriever
2. Jack Russell	German Shepherd
3. Staffordshire Bull Terrier	Beagle
4. Border Collie	Golden Retriever
5. Yorkshire Terrier	Yorkshire Terrier
6. Cocker Spaniel	Bulldog
7. German Shepherd	Boxer
8. Golden Retriever	Poodle
9. Greyhound/Whippet	Dachshund
10. Rottweiler	Rottweiler
11. Shi Tzu	Shi Tzu
12. King Charles Spaniel	Miniature Schnauzer
13. West Highland Terrier	Doberman Pinscher

Sources: UK and USA Kennel Clubs

Unhealthy?

In the early years of dog-breeding, ignorance and over-enthusiasm led to health and welfare problems for pedigree animals. Dogs bred purely for appearance, or for some other special feature, were often descended from only a few specimens. They therefore belonged to a dangerously small 'gene-pool' and were likely to inherit crippling deformities or diseases.

Today, irresponsible breeders still put greed, ambition or a search for novelty before animal welfare, although organisations such as the Kennel Clubs in Britain and the USA aim to educate breeders and customers. Activists say that the welfare of dogs and their right to lead a natural life are far more important than human fashions or preferences. And many, many dog lovers prefer to own a happy, healthy mongrel dog of unknown parentage than a sickly pedigree.

In 2005, the scientific world was shocked by the announcement that 'Snuppy' (**S**eoul **N**ational **U**niversity **Pu**ppy), the first cloned dog, had been born in South Korea. Snuppy was created by a team of 45 scientists using a cell from the ear of an Afghan Hound. The project took 3 years and involved 123 surrogate mother dogs; only 3 produced pups, and Snuppy was the only one to survive. Critics argued that the Snuppy experiment caused unjustified suffering to the dogs concerned. They also feared for the health of Snuppy himself, although he has survived for several years and fathered puppies.

In 2007, Koreans also created the first transgenic puppies, implanted with a gene that makes them glow red under ultraviolet light. In 2008, an American became the owner of the world's first commercially cloned puppies, created in a laboratory to replace her much-loved pet.

Odd dogs

• Basset Hounds, with their big bodies and short legs, cannot swim. Most other dogs are good swimmers, splashing through the water doing (what else?) the doggy-paddle.

• Dalmatians, famous for their spotted coats, are born pure white. Their spots develop as they get older, from around 3 weeks old.

• Basenjis, from Africa, are the only breed of dogs not to bark.

• Chow Chows, from east Asia, have blue or black tongues.

• St Bernard dogs, from the valleys of the Swiss Alps, often weigh more than a man.

• Dachshunds were bred with extra-short legs to attack badgers in their dens.

• Newfoundland dogs have webbed feet (to help them swim) and can use their tails like rudders.

• The Lundehund (puffin-hound) breed from Norway has developed polydactyly (extra toes). It usually has six toes on each foot. It can also fold its ears down to keep out moisture when swimming underwater. It was originally bred to hunt puffins, for food!

• Greyhounds are the fastest breed over short distances (up to around 800 m); Salukis are fastest over longer distances. Both can run at up to 42 mph (68 km/h) – very nearly as fast as a racehorse.

• The distinctive Poodle trim (topknot, tufts on legs and tail, lower body bare) may have originated to stop dogs getting waterlogged as they retrieved prey in lakes and marshes. The top-knot might also have been useful as a 'handle' if the dog got into difficulty in bogs or deep water.

"

Animals are such agreeable friends – they ask no questions, they pass no criticisms...

British novelist George Eliot (Mary Anne Evans)
(1819–1880)

"

CHAPTER NINE

DOGGONE

A non-offensive way of saying 'God-damn!'

Well, dogs may not talk, but people most certainly do. And a surprising number of their remarks refer to dogs, for good or for ill. Well-chosen compliments may make us as pleased as a dog with two tails. On the other hand, cruel or careless comments will make us feel like a dog's dinner or even as sick as a dog, whether they come from a lazy dog, a dog in the manger or a hostile person wishing to give a dog a bad name.

Just like our opinions of dogs themselves, dog words and phrases can be positive or negative, full of praise or blame. Some are direct and descriptive. Others use our poor old canine companions as similes or metaphors, likening dogs to everything from shining stars in summer skies to mustard-smeared sausages. So, without barking up the wrong tree, if we can avoid it, let's turn to look at some well-known doggy sayings:

Dog cheap Of little value, like an ordinary, old-fashioned, working dog.

Dog eat dog Ruthless competition. Although, in fact, dogs don't often eat other dogs. There is, however, a wonderfully chilling story by Jack London (1876–1916) about an Arctic pioneer, who, of course, has his dog with him. The pioneer has just three matches with which to light a fire that will keep him warm – and alive. His first two attempts fail. The third attempt lights a fire, but before long it is extinguished by a sudden flurry of snow. The pioneer knows he is doomed. Meanwhile, his dog looks on, hungrily... In fact, at the end of the story, the dog makes its way to the nearest human settlement, where it hopes it will find food. But the dying pioneer does not know that.

Dogfight Used during World Wars I and II to describe an airborne fight between pilots flying fast aircraft carrying guns.

Dog-house To be in the dog-house is to be in disgrace. A dog-house or kennel was usually a pretty miserable place.

Dog-Latin Rough, simple, clumsy Latin, spoken or written by poorly educated priests and people in Europe, between around AD 1000 and 1700. Another reference to dogs being humble and unimportant.

Dogleg A sharp bend, as in a dog's back leg. Often used to describe a roadway or boundary.

Dog's nose A strong but unsubtle drink. Wet, dark and allegedly comforting. A mixture of gin and beer.

Dog's sleep Rather strangely, the same as a catnap: a short sleep from which the sleeper wakens easily. It was traditionally said that dogs sleep with one eye open.

Dog-tags Set of metal tags or discs worn by soldiers in combat, giving (at a minimum) their name, enrolment number and religion.

Dog-tired Utterly exhausted. Wanting to flop down or curl up like a dog and fall asleep instantly.

Gay dog A pleasure-seeking, irresponsible, man-about-town. Flirtatious and definitely heterosexual. A relic of an age that now seems as far-distant as the pyramids.

Dead dog Something utterly worthless.

Dirty dog Someone untrustworthy; a double-crosser.

Help a lame dog over a stile Assist a person confronted by an obstacle of any kind.

Keep a dog and bark yourself Hire someone to work for you, but still do the job yourself. Harks back to the time when dogs were expected to work, as guards or lookouts.

Lie doggo To lie low, perhaps in hiding, like a dog that is frightened. Dog psychologists say that dogs can feel happiness, sadness, fear, anger and surprise, but not more complex emotions such as guilt or remorse.

Sea dog An old seaman, full of experience – and, very likely, tall tales.

See a man about a dog An excuse for leaving a meeting or social gathering early. Often, a euphemism for needing to visit the bathroom/lavatory, or for having some other engagement that you wish to keep secret.

Shaggy-dog story A supposedly humorous story, often told at great length with many additions and elaborations, and sometimes with an unexpected ending. Often, the tale is more amusing to the teller than to the listeners.

Sly dog A cunning, devious, secretive person.

Spotted dog or 'spotted dick'. Nickname for a steamed suet pudding containing dried currants, raisins or sultanas.

Letting the tail wag the dog Letting the least important person, or least significant element in a problem, take control.

Top dog Just as it says, the leading member of a group. But NB the note about supposed dog 'dominance' on pages 82–83.

Man bites dog

A saying among journalists, referring to an extraordinary or remarkable event – in other words, 'real news'. The reverse, 'Dog bites man' would not be worthy of comment. The originator of the phrase is not known for certain. Possibly it was British newspaper magnate Alfred Harmsworth, Lord Northcliffe (1856–1922), or John B. Bogart (1848–1921), editor of the *New York Sun*.

In 2007, international news agency Reuters ran the story: 'It's news! Man bites rabid dog in southern India.'

Hot dog

A sausage in a long bread roll, coated with mustard, tomato ketchup, relish or a myriad of different sauces. The 'dog' is made following different local recipes, using beef, pork, turkey and more, stuffed into natural (gut!) or artificial casings, then steamed, baked, boiled or fried. The roll is steamed or toasted, too, and sliced open along the side (more room for dressing and chopped onions) or slit along the top (a neater-to-eat 'top-loader'). As American as baseball and often eaten at a game. But how did this humble, wildly popular, delicacy get its name?

Readers, this is not a nice thing to say, but it's more than a little likely that some early sausages might have contained dog meat – in Germany, if not in the USA. Did German migrants carry this custom with them when they settled in their new, transatlantic homes? We cannot tell for certain. But there is plenty of evidence that, by the 1890s, hungry customers in American cities were asking for 'hot dog' sausage snacks.

Dog collar A starched white cloth collar fastened back-to-front, with the opening behind the head. Traditionally worn by clergymen, but also (in different colours, and with trimmings) a fashion item for women in Victorian times. Named after the heavy rope, chain or leather collar worn by dogs, or the decorative collars worn by lapdogs.

Dog-eared Simply descriptive: with the tips or corners bent over, like the ears of some dog breeds. Often used to describe something damaged or ill-used, for example a book with 'dog-eared' pages.

Doggy bag A container to carry away food paid for but uneaten at the end of a restaurant meal. To save face, it is often said that the leftovers are 'for the dog', but they are just as likely to be consumed by humans.

Dog-rose A variety of wild rose, with delicate pink and white flowers. The ancient Greeks believed that its roots cured the bite of wild dogs.

Dog Star, Dog Days

Sirius, the brightest star in the sky, is also known as the Dog Star. It forms part of the constellation Canis Major (the Great Dog). Since ancient Egyptian times, Sirius has been seen as a herald, and a warning. Its rising often marked the beginning of the annual flooding of the River Nile. Its appearance was therefore welcomed. However, the ancient Greeks and Romans believed that the Dog Star added its heat to the already scorching rays of the summer sun. The days when it first appeared (from around 3 to 11 August), were known as the Dog Days, and were believed to be an evil time:

> The Sea boiled, the Wine turned sour, Dogs grew mad, and all other creatures became languid; causing to man, among other diseases, burning fevers, hysterics, and phrensies.

J. Brady, *Clavis Calendaria (Key to the Calendar)*, 1815

The Romans sacrificed a dog to Sirius every year, hoping to make the Dog Days less dangerous.

Good luck – and living ghosts

On the whole, dogs are sensible, down-to-earth creatures, so perhaps it's not surprising that there are relatively few superstitions connected with them – compared with spookier, flightier creatures such as cats and birds. But a few have survived. Like most other folk beliefs, they deal with matters of everyday importance – the weather, the chance difficulties of life, romance – and death.

• It's unlucky to meet a barking dog early in the morning.

• Being followed by a strange dog will bring good luck – or is terribly unlucky. (It all depends where you live.)

• A strange dog calling at your house means that you will meet a new friend.

• A howling dog means that death is approaching.

• A dog with seven toes can see ghosts.

• A barking dog on St Andrew's Day (30 November) tells young girls where their husbands will come from.

• Three white dogs seen together (a very unusual occurrence) are lucky.

• A black dog (very widespread) is a sign of evil.

• A dog barking after midnight is seeing the ghosts of living people who will die soon.

• If your dog refuses to follow you, it's a sign that something bad will soon be coming your way.

• A dog eating grass foretells rain.

• Plans made while sitting near a dog-rose bush will always fail.

• To bring good fortune in the New Year, feed a dog with bread and then push it out of the house. It will take any bad luck away with it.

> " Near this Spot
> are deposited the Remains of
> one who possessed Beauty
> without Vanity,
> Strength without Insolence,
> Courage without Ferocity,
> and all the Virtues of Man
> without his Vices.
> This praise, which would be
> unmeaning Flattery
> if inscribed over human Ashes,
> is but a just tribute to the
> Memory of BOATSWAIN,
> a DOG...

Epitaph by Lord Byron at the grave of his pet
Newfoundland dog that died of rabies in 1808.

"

CHAPTER TEN

EVERY DOG MUST HAVE HIS DAY

In October 2012, a new book was published, cannily timed to appeal to the Christmas market. It's title? *Pudsey: My Autobidography* – and, yes, it was the life-story of a dog. Newspapers claimed that a very substantial sum had been paid as an advance for the work. After all, Pudsey (a 6-year-old, off-white, shaggy mongrel) had become a celebrity. His acrobatic dancing had won a national talent competition. An international visit and promotional tours were planned. Pudsey was a star.

Somewhat less starry-eyed than the publishers, in August 2012, the UK Kennel Club issued a ban on 'extreme' and 'unnatural' activities involving dogs. These included acrobatic dance and 'degrading' dog clothes or costumes. The Club feared that dog-owners hoping to repeat Pudsey's success story with their own pets would expose the animals to harm.

In the public eye

Pudsey is perhaps typical of his times: admired at first for some eye-catching skill, but soon just famous for being famous. Rather like Millie, the dog belonging to US president George H. W. Bush (in office 1989–1994), who was also said to have written an autobiography – it sold far better than the president's own life story. A surprising number of US presidents have kept dogs. There has even been dog diplomacy: in the 1960s, President Kennedy was rather pointedly given pups descended from early Soviet space-dogs (see pages 162–163). Some of his aides worried that they might have been bugged. More recently, around 2008, Russian President Putin was said to have made unflattering comparisons between his own large dog and President George W. Bush's smaller Scottish terrier, Barney. During World War II, the name of President Roosevelt's pet dog (Fala) was used as a secret army password. As that little list shows, Pudsey is far from being the first dog to have won fame – in real life or in fiction. And many other dogs' achievements have been rather more substantial.

Hero dogs

Since 1943, when the honour was created, 26 dogs have been awarded the Dickin Medal (administered by animal charity PDSA) – the canine equivalent of the Victoria Cross (Britain's highest human award for bravery). Often, hero dogs have belonged to the armed forces, but some have been civilians. A few suffered and died as martyrs to science. It is still debated whether their sufferings were necessary.

The most famous example of an armed forces dog is perhaps Judy, a pointer, who was ship's mascot on a Royal Navy gunboat in the Far East during World War II. She used her keen hearing to detect advancing enemy aircraft long before the sailors knew that danger was near. When her ship was eventually sunk, in 1942, Judy struggled ashore with the survivors. But the island where they landed was a desert and the men feared they would die of thirst, until Judy dug in the sand and found fresh water. When the wrecked sailors were captured by Japanese troops, Judy went with them, and was officially registered as a prisoner of war. In appalling conditions, she comforted the men, and helped distract the guards.

Judy and her fellow prisoners were shipwrecked once again, as they were being transferred to another prison. Again, Judy helped sailors to survive – and, as her closest human companion explained, 'gave them a reason to survive' in fresh and terrible captivity. Judy herself was condemned to death by Japanese guards, who planned then to cook her and feed her to the prisoners. For months, Judy hid in the jungle, surviving on rats, snakes and monkeys. Liberated at the end of the war, Judy was heard barking as part of British national radio's special victory broadcast.

In which we serve

Thousands of other dogs also served bravely in World Wars I and II; the special British Army Dog School, set up in 1942, trained around 7,000 animals during its first three years alone. Military dogs worked as messengers, detected hidden enemies, sniffed out landmines, rescued injured soldiers, attacked wouldbe assassins and even parachuted (with their own chutes) behind enemy lines. US Army dog Chips – a German Shepherd, Collie and Siberian Husky cross – was honoured for extraordinary courage in 1943. Under heavy fire, he chased four Italian machine-gunners out of a pillbox (miniature fort) and, the same day, although wounded, helped to capture ten prisoners.

There were many non-combatant dog mascots, too, and civilian dogs that worked with rescue teams in bombed cities, finding and helping to dig out people trapped under collapsed buildings. In 2010, Treo, a black Labrador bomb-detector dog who served with British forces in Afghanistan, became the latest dog to receive the Dickin Medal.

Dogs will be dogs

Huskies, sniffer dogs and even mountain rescue dogs (such as Barry, the Swiss St Bernard reputed to have saved 40 travellers lost in the Alps between 1800 and 1812) were all doing what came naturally, or else what their ancestors had been trained to do for centuries. Even Pickles, the 'hero dog' who found the solid-gold World Cup after it had been stolen in 1966, was only enjoying a typical doggy sniff around some bushes.

But in 1957, the world was amazed – and more than a little alarmed – to hear that Laika ('Barker'), a three-year-old mongrel from Russia, had been blasted into space on board

Soviet spacecraft *Sputnik II*. The experiment succeeded; for the first time, it showed that a living creature could withstand the stresses of a rocket launch and weightless earth orbit. But Laika died, probably just a few hours after take-off, from overheating.

Shock and outrage were the much stronger emotions that greeted news of secret 'smoking beagle' experiments, carried out from the 1950s to the 1970s in Britain and the USA. Captive dogs were forced to smoke up to 30 cigarettes per day, so that scientists could observe the damage caused by regular exposure to tobacco. Even today, according to PETA,* over 75,000 dogs per year are used in medical experiments in the USA. These studies will almost certainly help humans in developing new drugs and investigating common ailments shared by dogs and humans. A price worth paying?

*http://www.peta.org/issues/animals-used-for-experimentation/dogs-in-laboratories.aspx

A race for life

In 1925, before planes suitable for icy weather, or snowmobiles, had been invented, an epidemic of diphtheria threatened the remote Alaskan town of Nome. The only local doctor cabled that a million units of antitoxin (life-saving treatment) were urgently needed. But it was winter-time, and the only way of reaching Nome was by dog-sled, pulled by huskies. The weather was frightful (a blizzard); the distance was vast (over 1080 km/670 miles). Could the dogs get the antitoxin there in time?

Yes, they could! In a heroic dash through howling winds, nightmare ice and snow, relay teams of around 150 huskies, led by dogs Balto, Seppala and Togo, completed the journey in just five and a half days. Thanks to their toughness, endurance and obedience, hundreds of lives were saved.

Faithful friends

No account of hero dogs could be complete without a mention of Greyfriars Bobby – a small but devoted Skye Terrier who used to accompany his owner, Auld Jock Gray, into Edinburgh – until, in 1858, Jock died. Jock's body was buried in the Greyfriars kirkyard in Edinburgh. It was strictly out of bounds to dogs, but Bobby was determined to be with his master. Although repeated efforts were made to drive Bobby away, he was eventually given permission to stay close to his master's grave. Bobby spent 14 years at Greyfriars; thousands came to see him, including Queen Victoria. He died in 1872, and a statue was erected to his memory the following year.

Strange but true, from 1925 to 1934, Bobby's story – or something very similar – was re-enacted in Japan. Hachiko, a golden-brown Akita, was in the habit of waiting for his master at the train station every day, when he returned from work. After his master died, Hachiko refused to change his behaviour, but went to the station every day, until his own death nine years later.

Happiness is a warm puppy

As well as (supposedly) writing books, just like Pudsey and Millie, dogs have featured in thousands of novels, stories, poems, comic strips and their assorted spin-offs, all created by humans.

Some have been record-breakers. For example, American comic strip *Peanuts*, featuring beagle Snoopy, a dog who voiced the existential angst of the mid-20th century, was published from 1950 to 2000. Containing 17,897 episodes and attracting a readership of over 350 million, *Peanuts* has been called 'arguably the longest story ever told by one human being'. In 1969, Snoopy also became the world's first dog to have an Apollo lunar module named after him.

Cartoon (and other) heroes

In books from Belgium, first published in 1929, boy-detective Tintin was always accompanied by his dog Milou (in English, Snowy). In Scotland, Gnasher (born 1968), the suitably disreputable pet of comic hero Dennis the Menace, never spoke without a growl, spawned his own series, and sired puppies: Gnipper, Gnancy, Gnatasha, Gnaomi, Gnanette, and Gnora. Way back in 1904, children in the strangely sinister fairy story *Peter Pan* were guarded by a saintly Newfoundland, Nana. Enid Blyton's infamous 'Famous Five' had a faithful friend in the shaggy mongrel Timmy. Since 1969, the teenage *Mystery Gang* have enjoyed supernatural adventures, helped – or hindered – by Great Dane Scooby-Doo. In 1980, puppy Spot ('Dribbel' in Dutch; 'Smot' in Welsh) featured in the first-ever children's book with lift-up flaps, and created a whole new genre in juvenile publishing. *Spot* books have now sold over 50 million copies worldwide; *Tintin* has sold 200 million.

Stars of the silver screen

Although actors are often warned, 'Never work with children or animals,' some of Hollywood's most successful productions have featured dogs. Border Collie 'Lassie', played by a series of male dogs, starred in seven wholesome adventure films, starting with *Lassie Come Home* (1943). Long before Lassie, the first film with a dog as its hero was the British, black-and-white, silent *Rescued by Rover* (another Collie), made in 1905.

Lassie and Rover were both valued for genuinely canine qualities, but dogs as examples of good and bad human behaviour have also been the subjects of cartoon films, perhaps most successfully in *101 Dalmatians* (1996) and *Lady and the Tramp* (1955) – which was voted one of the 100 Best Love Stories of All Time by the American Film Institute, no less.

Viewers have been charmed by the gestures and expressions of non-speaking dog Gromit, companion of Wallace, in short films made for TV from 1989. They have also praised the perky performance of real-life Jack Russell 'Uggie', who steals many scenes in French rom-com *The Artist* (2011). Tim Burton's *Frankeenweenie*, about a boy who tries to use science to bring his dead pet dog back to life, was chosen to open the London Film Festival in 2012.

However, few films could match the real-life drama of German Shepherd Rin Tin Tin. Discovered as a starving puppy in a German dugout at the end of World War I, he was taken to the USA – and, in the words of his human biographer, went on to 'charm the world'. In America, he was trained by his ambitious but devoted owner, got his first part (as a wolf!), in a Hollywood silent film, starred in the epic *Where the North Begins* (1923), and made the first TV commercial for dog food. Four generations of his descendants had careers in film and TV. When he died, radio tributes were broadcast across the USA. Fame indeed!

"

Dogs are such fine
creatures that rare is the
man who desireth not one
for this purpose or
for that...

Gaston Phoebus, Count of Foix and Viscount of Béarn,
The Book of the Hunt, 1387–1388

"

CHAPTER ELEVEN

IN CONCLUSION

Today, we live in a world where (it is said) one in ten pets has appeared on social media of one sort or another, and a man in Scotland has claimed the protection of human rights law to allow him to live in a caravan with 46 Alsatians, as 'leader of the pack'.* At the same time, villagers in a remote Bulgarian village have revived the ancient pagan ritual of dog-spinning** in a desperate bid to remedy their dire economic situation, by magic.

---

* *The local Sheriff's words: see* The Herald, *26 September 2012.*
** *Dogs are suspended on a rope and spun round, before dropping into water. Villagers claim that the dogs are not hurt.*

An Australian city allegedly spent over A\$50,000 on a giant (5.5 x 8 m) dog-shaped recycled-wood interactive installation: FIDO (Fairfield Industrial Dog Object), although reportedly opposed by 90% of local residents. And the town of Rabbit Hash, Kentucky, USA, has been electing dogs as mayors since 1998. The present office-holder is a Border Collie named Lucy Lou.

Readers, it's a strange, strange world out there, and dogs are clearly part of it. They share our lives. They need us, and we most certainly need them.

Why oh why?

But why do we care so much about dogs, and lavish so much attention on them? Is it because dogs are famously faithful, and devoted to their owners? Or because they are energetic, hard-working and enthusiastic? After all, who could be more innocently delighted to see us than a dog? Or is it simply because dogs are useful, and beneficial?

Good for you...

In 2003, scientists reported the results of long-term studies that tried to find out whether pet owners led happier, healthier lives than people without pets. Over 11,000 responders took part, from Australia, China, Germany and other lands. The results were surprising, even to dog-lovers:

• People with pets were healthier than people without them.

• Pet-owners made almost 20% fewer visits to their doctors.

• Stroking a cat or dog slowed heartbeats and lowered blood-pressure; in other words, it reduced stress.

• Patients with a serious illness were more likely to recover if they had a pet.

In the UK, similar studies showed that:

• Children with pets are less likely to take time off school.

• Children with cats or dogs are less likely to suffer from hay fever, asthma or animal allergies.

In return…

In 2006/2007, the Animal Welfare Act introduced new legal duties for dog-owners, and the owners of all other pets, in England and Wales:

• providing suitable housing
• providing suitable food and water
• allowing pets to express normal behaviour
• protecting pets from illness and injury and providing treatment if required
• enabling pets to live with (or be protected from) other animals, as appropriate.

The Pact of the Fire

The Lakota Sioux people of North America tell an old, old, story. In the beginning, there was the land and the sky, the sun and the moon, the forests and the rivers, the night and the day, First Birds and First Animals, First Man, First Woman and First Dog. It was bitterly cold and snowy. First Dog had puppies, and dared not leave them to freeze while she hunted for food. At last, shivering and starving, First Dog crept over and spoke to First Woman, who was tending a fire:

> I am dying but I want my puppies to survive. If I give them to you, they will be your companions. They will guard you, hunt with you, love you and help you in any way they can. They will be loyal; they will never leave you. But in return, you must love them too, and feed them and give them shelter, and care for them like your own children.

Of course, First Woman agreed. First Man, also. Then, as First Dog crawled away to die, she panted a terrible warning:

> If you love my puppies and look after them, the world will go well for you. But if you mistreat or neglect them, all mankind will suffer – from famine and disease and wars and death and misery.

The more I see of man…

The origin of this quotation is unknown, but it was
possibly first written by witty and worldly-wise French
noblewoman, Madame de Sévigné (1626–1696).

First Dog did not entirely trust humans. But
she was willing to try. Another traditional
story, from the Sámi people of Finland and
northern Sweden, hints at a happier
relationship:

> Two dogs sat on a hill, looking at reindeer
> on the plain below. Anxious, harassed
> humans were rushing to and fro, trying to
> herd the deer but failing miserably. 'Shall we
> go and help them?' said one dog to the other.
> 'I think they need us.'

Without a doubt, dogs have been, and still are,
valued because they use their animal skills to
help an alien, human species. They can be
trained to assist people who cannot see or
cannot hear, and people with limited mobility.
They can open doors, carry bags, fetch mobile
phones, switch on the TV… Some dogs can
even warn owners before the onset of an
epileptic seizure. Others can smell dangerous

drugs or high explosives, and detect cancer and diabetes. They can find people lost on mountains or trapped by earthquakes. What is more, as the Sámi story says, dogs do all this eagerly, and with good will.

...the more I love dogs

Not everyone loves dogs, or even likes them, of course. Some people treat them appallingly. But, among those who do value their canine companions, what are their ultimate reasons? Because dogs show gratitude and courage? Because we can rely on them? Because they help us learn and come to terms with ourselves? Or do we love dogs simply because they predictably, eternally, reliably, unconditionally, seem really, really to care? As US President Truman (in office 1945–1953) was said to have remarked: 'If you want a friend in Washington, get a dog.'

That's probably good advice if you want a friend ANYWHERE...

Glossary

adapted Changed or evolved to fit a particular set of conditions.

affluent Wealthy.

anatomical Relating to the structure of a body.

ancestor Earlier generations of a human or animal family: parents, grandparents, great-grandparents and so on.

antitoxin Substance that fights against or neutralises the toxins (poisons) produced in the body by infections.

archaeologists People who study the phyiscal remains of the past.

barbarous Savage, less than human.

bestiaries Books written in the European Middle Ages about real or fabulous animals, with a strongly moral message.

canine Relating to dogs.

canine teeth Fangs (four, at the front of a dog's mouth).

carnassial teeth Shear-like teeth, found towards the back of a dog's mouth.

carpal pad Thick cushioned pad on the lower part of a dog's leg. Used for extra stability on slippery ground.

chordata Animals with a spinal cord.

clade Genetic group.

classify Describe and sort into sets.

clootie wells Natural spings of water where people traditionally left scraps of cloth as offerings to nature spirits; usually, they hoped for healing in return.

compassionate Kind and considerate.

concentrated Containing a high proportion of something (for example, energy) within a small volume.

conditioned Trained to respond in a predictable way to external signals or sensations.

corroborating Supporting and reinforcing.

crepuscular Most active in the dim light of dawn and twilight.

degenerate Weak, of bad breeding, corrupt.

delirious With a mind disordered by illness, often seeing things that are not there.

descendants People or animals born to the same parents, grandparents, great-grandparents and so on.

dew-claw Claw set apart from the rest of a dog's claws, rather like a human thumb. In most breeds, on the front legs only.

diabetes Disease that affects the body's ability to digest and metabolise sugars.

digestive enzymes Naturally occurring chemicals that act as catalysts, helping acids break down food in the stomach.

domesticated Evolved to live close to and co-operate with humans.

dominant Having or claiming power over another creature.

dunk Dip.

eardrum A thin membrane (skin) inside the ear. Sound waves make it vibrate, and these vibrations are transmitted by delicate structures within the ear, and by nerves, to the brain.

evolve Change slowly over time to adapt to changing ecological circumstances.

excavators Archaeologists who dig up the remains of the past.

excommunicated Banned from the Church's rituals, and thereby damned to eternal punishment in hell.

exotic Foreign, attractive, interesting.

fast-twitch muscles Types of muscle fibres that have evolved to enable very fast movement.

feral Previously domesticated animals that now live wild, with little or no contact with humans.

fibrous Full of thick, stringy strands or threads.

friars Christian men belonging to brotherhoods who live lives devoted to God. They work in the everyday world, rather than shut away in monasteries.

gait Way of walking or running.

gene A molecule (collection of atoms) that holds the information needed to build and maintain the cells of a living animal (or plant) and passes that information on to the next generation.

gene pool Small, closed group of ancestors who share similar genes.

genetically programmed Resulting from a particular combination of genes, that is, from a particular inheritance.

gentle High-class, of good breeding.

grove Clump of trees or small wood, usually with an area of clear land at the centre.

hackles Hairs at the back of a dog's neck (below the base of the skull).

icons Holy pictures, revered by members of Orthodox Christian Churches in Greece, Eastern Europe and Russia.

immutability Unchangeability.

incisors Teeth used for cutting and biting.

instinct Inherited behaviour.

inhale Breathe in.

insulate Cover thickly, to maintain a steady temperature and protect from either heat loss or overheating.

land bridge Area of dry sea-bed between two land masses left uncovered during past Ice Ages, when seas and oceans froze.

lèse majesté Disrespect shown to a king or queen; an ancient crime.

lubricant Substance that reduces friction between touching surfaces.

mitochondrial DNA Genetic material passed from mothers to their offspring.

molars Teeth at the back of a dog's mouth, used for crushing and grinding.

molecule A collection of atoms linked together in a particular combination to make a substance. For example, a water molecule is made of hydrogen and oxygen atoms.

nasal passages Spaces within the nose; air passes through them.

natural selection The theory that, in any natural situation, the creatures best fitted or adapted to their surroundings will survive and reproduce, passing their genes to the next generation. Sometimes summed up as 'survival of the fittest'.

Neanderthal An early type of human (*Homo sapiens neanderthalensis*) that lived in Europe and probably died out around 30,000 years ago.

omnivores Animals that have evolved to eat a wide

range of different foods. Dogs, pigs and humans are all omnivores.

Orthodox Group of Christian Churches in Greece, eastern Europe and Russia who follow the leadership of Patriarchs, instead of the Pope in Rome.

pedigree Ancestry that can be traced back for many generations; regarding dogs, also means bred from known ancestors of good quality.

perpetually Always, for ever.

pine marten A small mammal, related to foxes and looking rather like them but with shorter legs. Lives in northern Europe and preys on insects, reptiles, birds and smaller mammals.

predators Animals who kill and eat others to survive.

prey species Animals that are hunted and killed by predators.

pricked (ears) Alert and upright.

propagate Reproduce.

psychopomps Guides of dead souls.

rabies A deadly disease, caused by a virus. It attacks the brain. Can be spread by bites from infected mammals.

reflex An action that happens automatically; a dog (or human) cannot consciously control it.

retina Layer of light-sensitive cells at the back of the eye.

retracted Pulled back.

ritual Ceremony with a religious or magic purpose.

roasting spit Wooden or metal pole used to hold meat to be roasted above an open fire. When fitted to a treadmill wheel – in the past, worked by dogs – it is turned round and round, so the meat cooks evenly.

rustic From the countryside; relating to farming and to peasants or farm workers

salve Smoothing, soothing cream or ointment.

spasm Sudden shortening or tightening, for example of musles. Can be very painful.

stint Limit, restrict, be mean with.

stop The degree of angle change between a dog's skull and nasal bone near the eyes.

tamed Wild, but accustomed to living close to humans.

tapetum lucidum Reflective screen behind the retina in the eye.

vertebrae Bones of the spine.

wanton Immoral, naughty.

waterwheel A large wheel that could be turned by a dog, horse or donkey, to lift water from a well. Also, a wheel resting in running water, and turned by it to provide power for machinery.

whale eye The eye of a dog with the white showing; often a sign of fear.

zealous Very keen and energetic.

Dogs timeline

c.65,000,000 BC Miacids, remote ancestors of the dog family, live on earth.

c.42,000,000 BC Caniformia (or Canoidea), ancestors of wolves, bears, seals, sea lions, walruses, racoons, weasels and dogs, evolve from the Miacids.

c.42,000,000–32,000,000 BC Some members of the Caniformia evolve into a new family, the Canidae.

c.34,000,000 BC Caninae (direct ancestors of dogs) evolve from a branch of the Canidae family.

c.32,000,000 BC *Leptocyon*, ancestor of modern dogs, evolves among the Caninae.

c.12,000,000 BC *Eucyon* evolves from *Leoptocyon*.

c.9,000,000 BC *Eucyon* spreads from North America to Asia and Europe.

c.6,000,000 BC *Canis*, ancestor of wolves, coyotes, jackals and dogs, first evolves. Slowly, *Canis* learn to group themselves into packs, to hunt together.

c.6,000,000–3,500,000 *Canis* species spread from North America to Asia and Europe.

c.1,800,000 BC *Canis* begin to look like modern wolves.

c.1,000,000 BC *Canis etruscus* and *C. mosbachensis*, close ancestors of modern wolves, evolve in Europe.

c.300,000 BC *C. lupus*, the modern wolf, evolves in Europe.

c.150,000–60,000 BC Some wolves begin to live close to human settlements and lose their fear of humans.

c.130,000–40,000 BC Modern dogs (*C. lupus familiaris*) evolve as a subspecies of *C. lupus*.

c.33,000 BC Remains of 'almost dogs' close to human settlements in Siberia.

c.31,700 BC Remains of 'almost dogs' close to traces of human activity in caves in Belgium.

c.26,000 BC Footprints of boy and 'almost dog' close together in cave in France.

c.25,000–24,000 BC Drilled skull of 'almost dog' and jewellery made of dog-teeth in Czech Republic.

c.12,000 BC Human and dog remains deliberately buried close together in Germany.

c.11,000 BC *Canis lupus* (wolf) becomes the most widespread predator on earth.

c.11,000–9,000 BC Dogs live with first human farmers.

c.10,000–9,000 BC Elderly woman buried with puppy in her arms, in Palestine.

c.1500 BC Egyptian text describes pampered pet dog.

c.900 BC Hebrew wrongdoers 'thrown to the dogs'.

c.800 BC Greek poet Homer describes faithful hunting dog of hero Odysseus.

c.800 BC Greeks tell how Hades is guarded by a three-headed dog.

c.700 BC–AD 100 Celtic warriors and hunters own prize hounds; dogs also feature in Celtic myths, as messengers from the Otherworld and as guides for dead souls.

c.570 BC–AD 400 Greeks and Romans breed specialised dogs for hunting, herding and guarding houses.

c.500 BC Greek philosophers describe dogs according to their appearance, habitat and method of reproduction.

c.450 BC Evidence that Greeks are keeping small, white, fluffy pet dogs.

c.400 BC Greek physician Hippocrates recommends dog flesh as a cure; he also uses dogs to help in diagnosis.

c.330 BC Alexander the Great names city of Peritas after his dog.

206 BC–AD 200 Han dynasty rules China. Special small dogs are bred for emperors only.

c.100 BC From around this date, the Romans import prize hunting dogs from the British Isles. They also keep small pet lapdogs, and become very attached to them.

c.50 BC Roman leader Julius Caesar complains that women spend too much time with pet dogs and neglect their children.

c. AD 630 Prophet Muhammad and the holy Qur'an encourage Muslims to respect living creatures.

c.800–1100 Vikings believe that dogs will accompany brave heroes to Valhalla. They bury dogs in warriors' graves.

c.1000–1800 Dogs used for entertainment in cruel sports, such as bear-baiting.

c.1200 Scholar Gerald of Wales claims that being licked by a dog can heal. Other medieval writers make similar suggestions.

c.1220 Mongol emperor Genghis Khan reported to own 5,000 mastiffs.

c.1300 BC Christian friars put an end to the worship of dog-saint Guinefort, in France.

c.1400 English poet Chaucer describes pampered pet lapdogs.

Timeline

c.1450–1650 Artists use dogs to symbolise faithfulness, especially in marriage.

c.1480–1700 Small dogs sometimes accused of being witches' familiars (tame evil spirits). Many traditional tales of the devil appearing as a black dog first recorded around this time.

c.1500 Asian breeds of dog first introduced to Europe.

c.1500–1700 European kings and queens are famous dog-lovers.

c.1550–1750 European women use 'puppy water' as a beauty aid, and make gloves from dog-skin.

1570 English scholar Dr John Caius publishes book on British dogs. He describes three different types: gentle (for aristocratic sports and pets), working (on farms and as guard-dogs), degenerate (ordinary dogs, poor entertainers' dogs etc).

1665 One of the first-ever experiments in blood transfusion, in London, using dogs.

c.1750–1800 Attitudes towards dogs are changing, among scientists, thinkers, writers, poets, artists, and educated middle- and upper-class people.

c.1800 Napoleon removes the ears from his dog, to give it a fashionable appearance.

c.1815 onwards Breeders 'create' many new varieties of dogs. Exotic dog breeds are imported to Europe and the USA from Asia, Africa, the Middle East.

1824 First animal welfare organisation, the RSPCA, founded in London.

1858–1872 Dog 'Greyfriars Bobby' waits on his dead master's grave.

1859 Scientist Charles Darwin suggests that all dogs might be descended from the same ancestor.

1873 Kennel Club founded in UK.

c.1880 Queen Victoria, a great dog-lover, condemns cruelty to animals.

1884 American Kennel Club founded.

1901 Russian scientist Ivan Pavlov (1849–1936) shows that dogs can be conditioned to make reflex responses to signals (in Pavlov's experiment, a bell).

1902 Sir Arthur Conan Doyle publishes famous Sherlock Holmes detective story, *The Hound of the Baskervilles*.

1905 Film *Rescued by Rover*.

1923 First film starring German Shepherd *Rin Tin Tin*.

1925 Teams of dogs pull sleds carrying life-saving medical treatment to diphtheria sufferers in the Arctic.

1929 Story-books featuring Tintin and his dog Snowy first published.

1942 British Army Dog Training School set up.

1943 Film *Lassie Come Home*.

1943 Dickin Medal created, to honour animals that have show exceptional bravery. It has been won by many dogs.

1950 Charles M. Schulz's *Peanuts* cartoon, featuring Snoopy, a Beagle, first published.

1950s–1970s Controversial 'smoking Beagle' medical experiments in UK and USA.

1955 Film *Lady and the Tramp*.

1957 Russian mongrel Laika is the first dog sent into space.

1959 Russian scientist Dmitry Belayev begins 'Silver fox experiment'. He shows how wild creatures can be domesticated, and how they develop linked physical changes at the same time.

1989 First short film featuring dog Gromit (and human Wallace).

1996 Film *101 Dalmatians*.

1997 Genetics scientists show that all dogs are descended from the grey wolf, *Canis lupus*.

1998 US town Rabbit Hash, Kentucky, begins to elect dogs as mayors.

2000 Scientists query the 'dominance' theory popular with many dog trainers.

2002 Scientists show that dogs are better than chimpanzees at interpreting signals made by humans.

2005 SNUPPY, the first cloned dog, born in South Korea.

2005 Dog Surfing Championships begin in California.

2007 First transgenic dog created, in South Korea.

2007 Animal Welfare Act places new duties on dog-owners in the UK.

2010 Around 4.7 million people in the USA are bitten by dogs.

2010 Italian researchers show that dogs can recognise their owners' faces.

2011 World-record price paid for pedigree Tibetan Mastiff in China.

2012 Dancing dog wins national TV talent contest in the UK.

2012 Worldwide protests by animal rights activists during Bok-Nal annual dog-eating festival in Korea.

2012 Newspapers worldwide report that a starving boy in India survived by drinking milk from a feral dog.

Index

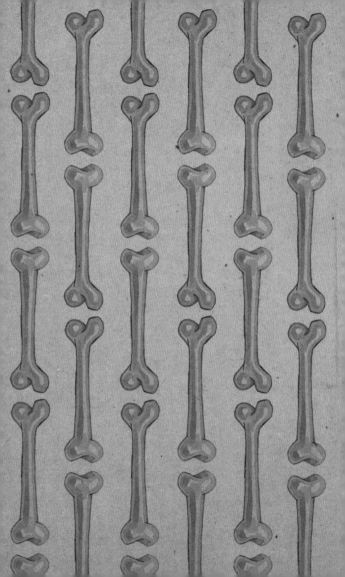